Empowering Women in the Transition Towards Green Growth in Greece

OECD

BETTER POLICIES FOR BETTER LIVES

This document, as well as any data and map included herein, are without prejudice to the status of or sovereignty over any territory, to the delimitation of international frontiers and boundaries and to the name of any territory, city or area.

The statistical data for Israel are supplied by and under the responsibility of the relevant Israeli authorities. The use of such data by the OECD is without prejudice to the status of the Golan Heights, East Jerusalem and Israeli settlements in the West Bank under the terms of international law.

Please cite this publication as:
OECD (2022), *Empowering Women in the Transition Towards Green Growth in Greece*, OECD Publishing, Paris, https://doi.org/10.1787/a9eacee6-en.

ISBN 978-92-64-88818-0 (print)
ISBN 978-92-64-40076-4 (pdf)
ISBN 978-92-64-56025-3 (HTML)
ISBN 978-92-64-51645-8 (epub)

Foreword

This report offers policy advice to Greece on building interlinkages between its national environmental policies, and gender equality policies, under the gender-environment nexus. It builds on a related report, *Gender and the Environment: Building Evidence and Policies to Achieve the SDGs* (2021), which explored the links between gender equality and environmental sustainability in the context of Agenda 2030, applying an integrated policy framework taking into account both inclusive growth and environmental considerations.

An integrated approach to gender equality and environmental sustainability could help to improve women's economic empowerment and enhance women's roles in environmental sustainability and green growth. Likewise, enhancing gender equality and women's economic empowerment and decision-making can lead to better environmental and climate outcomes and policies. Taking into account the specific needs, preferences and well-being of women, as well as their position due to intersectional factors related to environmental and climate policies, helps to identify the trade-offs and complementarities between gender equality and environmental goals. Gender mainstreaming in environmental policies could also lead to transformative actions supporting women's economic empowerment.

This report assesses environmental and climate policies through a gender lens, and gender equality policies through an environmental lens. It focuses on policies and measures that could support women's economic empowerment in environment-related sectors; women's environmental leadership and decision making; and mainstreaming gender equality and environmental sustainability in policy tools. It proposes a series of recommendations that, if taken on board, could support integrating the gender-environment nexus into Greece's national policies.

The OECD gratefully acknowledges the Greek Ministry of Labour and Social Affairs for financial support and co-operation in providing information and facilitating contacts inside and outside government institutions. A special appreciation also to the Greek Ministry of Environment and Energy for the information provided.

The author of this report, and overall co-ordinator, is Dimitra Xynou (OECD Environment Directorate). Sara Ramos Magaña and Helene Bendig provided background research (OECD Environment Directorate). Kumi Kitamori, Acting Environment Deputy Director, and Sigita Strumskyte, Co-ordinator, Sustainable Development & Gender, provided oversight and guidance. Preparation of this report benefited from review and comments from Willem Adema, Valentina Patrini (ELS) and Jacobo Garcia Villarreal (GOV). Amelia Smith (OECD Environment Directorate) provided editorial advice. Beth Del Bourgo and William Foster provided communications support.

The OECD Working Party on Environmental Performance reviewed a draft version of this report, which was also shared with the Working Party on Gender Mainstreaming and Governance, and the Employment, Labour and Social Affairs Committee. It was declassified by the Environment Policy Committee after being shared for information.

Table of contents

FIGURES

TABLES

BOXES

Acronyms and abbreviations

AI	Artificial Intelligence
ALS	Alternative management system
APGPP	Action Plan for Green Public Procurement
C3E	Clean Energy Education and Empowerment
CAP	Common Agricultural Policy
CEAP	Circular Economy Action Plan
CEDAW	Convention on the Elimination of all Forms of Discrimination Against Women
CEDEFOP	European Centre for the Development of Vocational Training
CO_2	Carbon dioxide
COP	Conference of the Parties
EEGS	Environmental Goods and Services Sector
ESCO	European Skills, Competences, Qualifications and Occupations
ETS	Emissions Trading System
EU	European Union
FPDS	Federal Procurement Data System
GBVAWG	Gender based violence against women and girls
GEAP	Gender Equality Action Plan
GHG	Greenhouse gas
GIL4W	Greek Innovation lab for women
GPP	Green public procurement
GSDFPGE	General Secretariat for Demography, Family Policy and Gender Equality
ICT	Information and Communication Technologies
ILO	International Labour Organisation
INDAP	National Institute for Agricultural Development, Chile
IRENA	International Renewable Energy Agency
IT	Information technology
JTDP	Just Transition Development Plan

LULUCF	Land use, land-use change and forestry
MIT	Massachusetts Institute of Technology
MoEE	Greek Ministry of Environment and Energy
MW	Megawatt
NECP	National Energy and Climate Plan
NISA	National Innovation and Science Agenda, Australia
NGO	Non-governmental organisation
NSC	National Skills Council
NSCCA	National Strategy for Climate Change and Adaptation
NSE	Natural sciences and engineering
OAED	Greek Manpower Employment Organisation
O*NET	Occupational Information Network
PRODEMU	Foundation for the Promotion and Development of Women, Chile
R&D	Research and development
RES	Renewable Energy Systems
RIA	Regulatory impact assessment
RRF	Recovery and Resilience Facility
SAGE	Science in Australia Gender equity
SDG	Sustainable Development Goal
SEV	Hellenic Federation of Enterprises
SIGI	Social Institutions and Gender Index
SME	Small and medium sized enterprise
STEM	Science, technology, engineering and mathematics
UNFCCC	United Nations Framework Convention on Climate Change
UNIDO	United Nations Industrial Development Organisation
WBL	Women, Business and the Law Index
WISE	Women in STEM and Entrepreneurship, Australia

Executive summary

Gender equality and environmental sustainability, the two components of the gender-environment nexus, require immediate action at national and international levels. The environmental and climate crises and social inequalities exacerbated by the COVID-19 pandemic have prompted countries to increase action on both fronts. Yet an integrated approach is often lacking, with countries missing the opportunity to explore trade-offs and complementarities between gender equality and environmental sustainability, and to minimise potential negative impacts of environmental and climate policies.

Greece is addressing gender considerations in policy-making, with an emphasis on women's economic empowerment, women's active participation in decision-making, and eliminating gender-based violence against women and girls (GBVAWG). In parallel, Greece, as other European Union member states, is prioritising the transition towards a net-zero economy, introducing environmental and climate strategies and policies to support this objective. The gender-environment nexus is still largely absent in Greece's national policies, however. An assessment of the country's national policies shows that there is great potential to introduce the gender-environment nexus into existing policy initiatives, which would support Greece's shift towards green growth and advance women's economic empowerment.

An assessment of Greece's environmental and climate policies through a gender lens shows that there is no systematic application of the gender-environment nexus in policy design or implementation. Social considerations are largely taken into account when preparing national environmental and climate-related policies, but there is no explicit gender approach. Issues such as tackling women's energy poverty, introducing gender-sensitive climate adaptation in urban design, and applying gender-sensitive environmental impact assessments, are absent. At the same time, women's role in phasing out fossil fuel dependency is partly recognised, with targeted measures linked to women's employment being introduced. This is also the case for women's role in sustainable agriculture and forestry. More strategically supporting women in STEM studies and careers, and supporting them in reaching leadership positions, could increase the number of women in traditionally male-dominated sectors such as eco-innovation and green patenting. In the case of circular economy, supporting women's inclusion in green entrepreneurship, promoting gender-sensitive green public procurement, and taking account of female behavioural preferences and consumption patterns in policy design and implementation could lead to more sustainable choices.

Assessment of Greece's gender equality policies through an environmental sustainability lens highlights the need for more explicit actions to empower women in the green economy. Targeted approaches to green skills and vocational training, to science and technology programmes, and to gender-sensitive green recovery measures, could increase women's presence in green occupations. Further mainstreaming gender in sectoral policies, such as in data collection and building gender-sensitive environmental statistics, as well as introducing gender budgeting and financing, could better reflect the differentiated environmental impacts for policies by gender. Finally, guaranteeing women's participation in public consultation and decision-making could increase emphasise women's role as agents of change in environmental and climate policy.

Integrating the gender-environment nexus into national policies requires tools and initiatives that mainstream gender in sectoral policies and enhance women's role in the economy and society. This report includes a series of recommendations that, if implemented, could further enhance the synergies from integrating gender equality and environmental sustainability goals. Structured under five target areas – mainstreaming gender in environmental policies; empowering women in environmental sectors; supporting women's presence in environmental leadership and decision-making; promoting gender-sensitive environmental justice; and building up statistical data to monitor progress – these recommendations could be useful not only to Greece but also to other countries that wish to integrate the gender-environment nexus into their national policies. For each policy area analysed, examples of how this approach has been successful in other OECD countries.

1 Introducing the gender-environment nexus in the case of Greece

This chapter presents the gender-environment nexus and proposes a policy framework that could be introduced by Greece and other countries wishing to coherently integrate gender equality and environmental sustainability into their national policy making. It gives an overview of the analysis and methodology used to prepare this report, including limitations due to insufficient data.

1.1. The gender-environment nexus

Gender equality and environmental sustainability are gaining political momentum as global challenges that require urgent action at the national and international levels. The profound global shock created by the COVID-19 pandemic risks undoing recent progress made on both objectives.

The COVID-19 pandemic has had a higher mortality rate among men, but its economic and social impacts have disproportionately affected women. Women face compounded challenges: a high share in the front-line healthcare workforce, putting them at risk of infection; increased unpaid care work in households; high risk of increased economic insecurity (both now and in the future); and increased risk of violence, exploitation, abuse or harassment during times of crisis and quarantine (OECD, 2020[1]).

The recent COVID-19 pandemic along with the ongoing environmental and climate crises provide an opportunity for countries to prioritise gender equality and women's economic empowerment, and environmental and climate action, into their economic recovery measures. This approach could also bring wider benefits beyond the pandemic.

Building on the interlinkages between gender equality and environmental sustainability provides the basis for a more coherent approach to addressing gaps and inconsistencies in policy making. National recovery measures need to align with international commitments, such as the Convention on the Elimination of all Forms of Discrimination Against Women (CEDAW), the 1995 Beijing Declaration and Platform for Action, the 2015 Paris Agreement on Climate Change, and the United Nations' Agenda 2030 for Sustainable Development (2030 Agenda).

Gender equality and environmental sustainability figure prominently, though separately, in the United Nations 2030 Agenda, in Sustainable Development Goal 5 (SDG5: Achieve gender equality and empower all women and girls) and the five Planet Goals (SDGs 6, 12, 13, 14 and 15).[1] Identifying the interactions between these goals could help to maximise synergies and complementarities and, where there are trade-offs, minimise their negative impacts on sustainable development (OECD, 2021[2]).

The gender-environment nexus recognises the extent to which slow progress on environmental measures affects the condition of women and men differently and hampers gender equality. It brings to the forefront how gender equality and the empowerment of women and girls can deliver positive impacts on the environmental aspects of certain policies (OECD, 2021[2]). An integrated approach to gender equality and environmental sustainability could alleviate limitations to gender equality and women's economic empowerment deriving from existing social, cultural discrimination and biases; and could enhance women's role towards environmental sustainability and green growth.

The OECD's analysis on the economic and well-being benefits of integrating gender equality and environmental targets and policies (OECD, 2021[2]) indicates that:

- Ensuring a just transition to low-carbon economies for men and women can increase productivity and lead to better economic outcomes and more resilient societies. Enhancing the participation of women in green innovation can be a source of high-skilled jobs for women and boost overall productivity.
- Sustainable infrastructure (i.e. transport, energy, water, etc.) that considers women's needs is key for enhancing their economic empowerment and labour force participation. Designing environmentally conscious infrastructure with a gender lens would provide win-win outcomes for all and improve well-being across the population.
- Incorporating a gender lens into public policies such as green product labelling, public information campaigns and targeted education programmes can help accelerate women's contribution towards more sustainable consumption patterns and boost the overall sustainability of production and consumption.

1.2. The OECD's gender equality framework

The OECD provides policy guidance for addressing gender inequality, and tackling some of the barriers and limitations faced by women and girls, through two Recommendations:

- The _OECD Recommendation on Gender Equality in Public Life_ (2015), focuses on effective governance and accountability for gender equality; closing leadership gaps in public life; and equal access to public employment. It recommends that Adherents strengthen accountability and oversight mechanisms for gender equality and mainstream initiatives across and within government bodies. It also provides actionable guidelines to enhance women's equal access to opportunities in service and judicial appointments (OECD, 2016[3]). The Recommendation is complemented by the _OECD Toolkit on Implementing and Mainstreaming Gender Equality_, which presents good practices to support countries in the implementation of the 2015 Gender Recommendation (OECD, 2018[4]).

- The _OECD Recommendation of the Council on Gender Equality in Education, Employment, and Entrepreneurship_ (2013), sets out measures that Adherents should consider implementing in order to address gender inequalities in education, employment and entrepreneurship. In particular, it recommends that Adherents should – through appropriate legislation, policies, monitoring, and campaigning – ensure equal access to education; better enable female labour force participation; promote family-friendly policies; foster greater male uptake of unpaid work; work toward better gender balance in positions of public and private sector leadership; and promote entrepreneurship among women (OECD, 2017[5]).

The OECD monitors countries' progress on implementing these Recommendations and extending their approaches to sectoral policies such as environmental and climate policies. Recent analysis shows that while most OECD countries do have a national strategy or action plan on gender equality or mainstreaming, there is no unified approach to addressing the nexus within environmental and climate policy making. A 2019 OECD survey on integrating gender in environmental policies showed that only 5 out of 28 responding countries "always" consider gender aspects in environmental policies, while 16 do so "occasionally". OECD countries are considering gender equality when developing policies on climate change, green entrepreneurship and green jobs, as well as on agriculture and forestry (OECD, 2020[6]).

1.3. An integrated gender-environment policy framework

Ensuring an equal role for women in sustainable growth is fair and constitutes environmentally, socially and economically responsible behaviour (OECD, 2021[2]). Gender equality and the inclusion of more women in the green labour force would benefit the transition to a low-carbon economy. Yet, gender equality is rarely prioritised in policies on infrastructure or urban development, energy, research and innovation, or sustainable consumption.

Introducing gender equality and women's economic empowerment in environmental and climate policies can lead to better policies in these fields. Women's and men's differentiated experiences with the environment are often overlooked, which can lead to less effective policies introduced for half of the population. Gender-sensitive and gender-responsive policies would be more inclusive, covering issues of vulnerability related to energy efficiency and energy poverty, climate change, biodiversity, agriculture, etc., or even of opportunity for better policy results (OECD, 2021[2]). Moreover, including more women in decision-making and leadership positions around the environment, whether in the public or private sector, could bring about more sustainable decisions and actions (Strumskyte, Ramos Magaña and Bendig, 2022[7]). Finally, considering countries' international commitments on gender equality and environmental policies, enhancing coherence between the two policy areas would help reorient national priorities in the long term.

1.4. The case of Greece - Introducing the gender-environment nexus

Greece currently addresses gender considerations in policy making in three main areas: (i) eliminating gender-based violence; (ii) reinforcing women's economic empowerment; and (iii) ensuring women's participation in decision making. A comprehensive legal framework has been introduced to this end, but many steps remain to fully implement it and to apply gender mainstreaming in policy making across different policy domains.

Current Impact assessments of environmental and climate policies in Greece do not take gender considerations into account. Gender equality priorities such as women's economic empowerment and leadership are often not well integrated into measures across policy domains, lacking targeted sectoral action that could improve women's presence in environment-related economic activities.

Recent policy initiatives, especially during the COVID-19 recovery period, show that Greece, along with other EU member states, is prioritising the transition towards a net-zero economy. Gender equality is also built into the methodology that will provide social expenditure information on EU member states' recovery plans under the EU Recovery and Resilience Facility (RRF), the main financial instrument. Greece is currently prioritising gender equality by introducing reforms and investments that also address gender-relevant challenges. The gender-environment nexus is still largely absent in Greece's national policies, however.

To support Greece's interest in introducing an integrated gender-environment policy framework, the OECD has assessed the country's existing policies, highlighting complementarities and trade-offs, as well as possible benefits that could support Greece's shift towards green growth.

1.4.1. Methodology

The following methods were used to introduce the gender-environment nexus in Greece's national policies: (i) mapping the gender-environment nexus, (ii) evaluating the impact of environmental policies on gender equality and women's empowerment, and (iii) assessing whether gender equality policies advance environmental sustainability. This methodology could support Greece and other countries that wish to systematise their policy approaches, identify gaps and challenges, and develop and use indicators to evaluate future policy making under the gender-environment nexus.

This report analyses the following Greek national strategies, policies, and policy tools:

- National Energy and Climate Plan
- National Action Plan against Energy Poverty
- Just Transition Development Plan
- National Strategy for Climate Change Adaptation
- Circular Economy Action Plan
- National Biodiversity Strategy and Action Plan

They were assessed based on their implicit or explicit impact on gender equality and women's economic empowerment. Analysis was conducted using existing evidence, research and data (where available). This is complemented by case studies and examples of how gender-differentiated impacts of environmental measures have been addressed in other OECD countries.

This report also examines Greece's Gender Equality Action Plan (GEAP) through an environmental lens, analysing gender equality policy priorities that cover supporting women's economic empowerment in the green economy, increasing women's participation in public life through leadership positions, and mainstreaming gender in sectoral policies, such as budgeting and impact assessments, including data collection.

1.4.2. Methodological limitations

Challenges do exist. As indicated in previous OECD work, sex-aggregated data on member countries' environmental policies and green growth is limited. It is usually collected through time series surveys, which are costly and hence only collected about every ten years. Insufficient data makes it difficult to thoroughly evaluate the benefits of integrating the gender-environment nexus into specific policies.

Furthermore, the analysis attempts to apply an intersectional approach, based on available data. Grouping women and girls into a single category does not allow for a full representation of the differentiated impact that other factors, in addition to gender, may have. Women and girls may face diverse situations of exclusions and opportunities based on income, age, location and other socio-economic characteristics that should also be taken into consideration when designing policies.

Efforts to integrate the gender-environment nexus into policy making may expose deep-rooted gender inequalities based on cultural or other barriers. The reasoning behind these are beyond the scope of this report. The approach selected is limited to the interlinkages between gender equality and environmental sustainability, and therefore only highlights gaps that may exist in policy making, with the aim of overcoming social norms, practices and cultural barriers through gender mainstreaming in environmental policies. It also touches upon key issues such as advancing women's leadership positions in environment-related decision making, and women's economic empowerment in environment-related economic sectors.

Finally, the analysis related to women's economic empowerment and inclusion in the green economy is not only limited to environmental sectors, i.e. economic sectors that generate environmental products such as goods and services produced for environmental protection or resource management. It also looks into environment-related economic sectors and activities, i.e. economic sectors and activities that may have an environmental impact and where a green transition could be an option.

1.4.3. Targets and structure

Analysis in this report aims at identifying policy recommendations that, if implemented, could help Greece achieve the following targets:

- Gender mainstreaming in environmental and climate policies;
- Women's economic empowerment in male-dominated environmental sectors;
- Women's presence in environmental leadership and decision-making;
- Gender-sensitive environmental justice;
- Statistical data and monitoring progress in integrating the gender-environment nexus.

Chapter 2 analyses the extent to which gender equality and women's economic empowerment are integrated into Greece's environmental and climate policies and tools. Chapter 3 assesses gender equality policies and their role in advancing environmental sustainability in Greece. Based on the analysis conducted in the previous chapters, Chapter 4 presents a series of recommendations that Greece could introduce in order to better integrate the gender-environment nexus into its national policy framework and further enhance the complementarities of reaching both the goals of gender equality and environmental sustainability.

References

Agroinformacion (2022), "La Rioja fomenta la igualdad de género, el relevo generacional y la sostenibilidad en su Ley de Agricultura y Ganadería", *agroinformacion.com*, https://agroinformacion.com/la-rioja-fomenta-la-igualdad-de-genero-relevo-generacional-y-sostenibilidad-en-su-ley-de-agricultura-y-ganaderia/ (accessed on 18 January 2022). [56]

Aragón, F., J. Rud and G. Toews (2018), "Resource shocks, employment, and gender: Evidence from the collapse of the UK coal industry", *Labour Economics*, Vol. 52, pp. 54-67, https://doi.org/10.1016/j.labeco.2018.03.007. [29]

Ashenmiller, B. (2011), "The Effect of Bottle Laws on Income: New Empirical Results", *The American Economic Review*, Vol. 101/3, pp. 60-64, http://www.jstor.org/stable/29783715. [86]

Atlason, R., D. Giacalone and K. Parajuly (2017), "Product design in the circular economy: Users' perception of end-of-life scenarios for electrical and electronic appliances", *Journal of Cleaner Production*, Vol. 168, pp. 1059-1069, https://doi.org/10.1016/j.jclepro.2017.09.082. [88]

Ayuntamiento de Madrd (2019), *Propuesta de fincionamiento del foro Madrd solicaria durante el ejercicio 2019*, https://www.madrid.es/UnidadesDescentralizadas/FondosEuropeos/madrid_es/EspecialInformativo/Cooperacion%20internacional%20desarrollo/Fichero/propuesta_funcionamiento_FMS_2019.pdf (accessed on 17 January 2022). [28]

Botta, E. (2019), "A review of "Transition Management" strategies: Lessons for advancing the green low-carbon transition", *OECD Green Growth Papers*, No. 2019/04, OECD Publishing, Paris, https://doi.org/10.1787/4617a02b-en. [97]

Bové, H. et al. (2019), "Ambient black carbon particles reach the fetal side of human placenta", *Nature Communications*, Vol. 10/1, https://doi.org/10.1038/s41467-019-11654-3. [16]

Bulut, Z., F. Kökalan Çımrin and O. Doğan (2017), "Gender, generation and sustainable consumption: Exploring the behaviour of consumers from Izmir, Turkey", *International Journal of Consumer Studies*, Vol. 41/6, pp. 597-604, https://doi.org/10.1111/ijcs.12371. [84]

C3E International and IEA (2019), *Status Report on Gender Equality in the Energy Sector*, https://www.cleanenergyministerial.org/sites/default/files/2019-06/Status%20Report%20on%20Gender%20Equality%20in%20the%20Energy%20Sector_0.pdf. [64]

Carlsson Kanyama, A., J. Nässén and R. Benders (2021), "Shifting expenditure on food, holidays, and furnishings could lower greenhouse gas emissions by almost 40%", *Journal of Industrial Ecology*, Vol. 25/6, pp. 1602-1616, https://doi.org/10.1111/jiec.13176. [22]

CBD (n.d.), *Aichi Biodiversity Targets*, https://www.cbd.int/sp/targets/ (accessed on 2 February 2022). [92]

Chateau, J., R. Bibas and E. Lanzi (2018), "Impacts of Green Growth Policies on Labour Markets and Wage Income Distribution: A General Equilibrium Application to Climate and Energy Policies", *OECD Environment Working Papers*, No. 137, OECD Publishing, Paris, https://doi.org/10.1787/ea3696f4-en. [103]

Chateau, J. and E. Mavroeidi (2020), "The jobs potential of a transition towards a resource efficient and circular economy", *OECD Environment Working Papers*, No. 167, OECD Publishing, Paris, https://doi.org/10.1787/28e768df-en. [96]

Chiappini, S. and M. De Rosa (2011), "Consuming rural development policies: Are there gender differences in Italian agriculture?", *Agricultural Economics Review*, Vol. 12/1, https://doi.org/10.22004/ag.econ.178214. [51]

Czap, N. et al. (2018), "Conforming to or defying gender stereotypes? Empathy nudging vs. financial incentives in environmental context", *Papers in Natural Resources*, Vol. 981, https://digitalcommons.unl.edu/natrespapers/981. [26]

Diehl, K. and P. Cerny (2021), *Women on the Move: Sustainable Mobility and Gender*, https://eu.boell.org/en/women-on-the-move-sustainable-mobility-and-gender (accessed on 1 February 2022). [36]

Dinis, I. et al. (2015), "Organic agriculture values and practices in Portugal and Italy", *Agricultural Systems*, Vol. 136, pp. 39-45, https://doi.org/10.1016/j.agsy.2015.01.007. [50]

DISER (n.d.), "Advancing Women in STEM strategy", *Australian Government, Department of Industry, Science, Energy and Resources*, https://www.industry.gov.au/data-and-publications/advancing-women-in-stem-strategy (accessed on 13 January 2022). [60]

Djoudi, H. et al. (2016), "Beyond dichotomies: Gender and intersecting inequalities in climate change studies", *Ambio*, Vol. 45/S3, pp. 248-262, https://doi.org/10.1007/s13280-016-0825-2. [9]

DoAFM (2021), *Minister McConalogue announces supports to promote gender equality in farming*, https://www.gov.ie/en/press-release/c9232-minister-mcconalogue-announces-supports-to-promote-gender-equality-in-farming/ (accessed on 12 January 2022). [54]

EC (2021), *Commission Staff Working Document on the territorial just transition plans*, https://ec.europa.eu/regional_policy/sources/thefunds/jtf/swd_territ_just_trans_plan_en.pdf. [30]

EC (2021), *GPP National Action Plans*, https://ec.europa.eu/environment/gpp/action_plan_en.htm (accessed on 16 January 2022). [76]

EC (2016), *Buying green! A handbook on green public procurement*, https://doi.org/10.2779/246106. [74]

EC (n.d.), *European Climate Law*, https://ec.europa.eu/clima/eu-action/european-green-deal/european-climate-law_en (accessed on 29 April 2022). [14]

EIGE (n.d.), *Agriculture and rural development*, https://eige.europa.eu/gender-mainstreaming/policy-areas/agriculture-and-rural-development. [47]

EmpowerMed (n.d.), *EMPOWERING WOMEN TO TAKE ACTION AGAINST ENERGY POVERTY*, https://www.empowermed.eu/ (accessed on 15 January 2022). [27]

Field, C. (ed.) (2014), *Climate Change 2014: Impacts, Adaptation, and Vulnerability. Summaries, Frequently Asked Questions, and Cross-Chapter Boxes. A*, World Meteorological Organization, https://www.ipcc.ch/site/assets/uploads/2018/03/WGIIAR5-IntegrationBrochure_FINAL-1.pdf. [10]

FIT (n.d.), *Finacial Literacy and New Business Models to Boost Women Entrepreneurship Possibilities*, https://the-fitproject.eu/. [72]

Gkasouka, M. and X. Foulidi (2018), *The Greek farmer woman: Capturing participation, problems, challenges and policy proposals to encourage women's participation in the agricultural sector and greek rural areas*, National Printing House, https://isotita.gr/wp-content/uploads/2018/02/%CE%97-%CE%95%CE%BB%CE%BB%CE%B7%CE%BD%CE%AF%CE%B4%CE%B1-%CE%B1%CE%B3%CF%81%CF%8C%CF%84%CE%B9%CF%83%CF%83%CE%B1.pdf. [45]

Green Industries SA (n.d.), *Women in Circular Economy Leadership Award*, https://www.greenindustries.sa.gov.au/women-in-ce-leadership-award (accessed on 11 January 2022). [89]

Grünewald, P. and M. Diakonova (2020), "Societal differences, activities, and performance: Examining the role of gender in electricity demand in the United Kingdom", *Energy Research & Social Science*, Vol. 69, https://doi.org/10.1016/j.erss.2020.101719. [21]

Hossain, M. et al. (2017), "Women in the boardroom and their impact on climate change related disclosure", *Social Responsibility Journal*, Vol. 13/4, pp. 828-855, https://doi.org/10.1108/srj-11-2016-0208. [61]

Huddart Kennedy, E., H. Krahn and N. Krogman (2015), "Are we counting what counts? A closer look at environmental concern, pro-environmental behaviour, and carbon footprint", *Local Environment*, Vol. 20/2, https://doi.org/10.1080/13549839.2013.837039. [20]

IEA (2020), *Gender diversity in energy: what we know and what we don't know*, https://www.iea.org/commentaries/gender-diversity-in-energy-what-we-know-and-what-we-dont-know (accessed on 23 March 2021). [63]

ILO (2015), *Gender equality and green jobs*, International Labour Organization. [70]

IRENA (2019), *Renewable energy: A gender perspective*, IRENA, http://www.irena.org. [59]

IUCN (n.d.), *Greece*, https://www.iucn.org/regions/europe/resources/country-focus/greece (accessed on 1 February 2022). [90]

Jerneck, A. (2018), "What about Gender in Climate Change? Twelve Feminist Lessons from Development", *Sustainability*, Vol. 10/3, p. 627, https://doi.org/10.3390/su10030627. [8]

Johnsson-Latham, G. (2007), *A study on gender equality as a prerequisite for sustainable development*, Report to the Environment Advisory Council, Stockholm, http://www.sou.se/mvb/. [81]

Kaenzig, J., S. Heinzle and R. Wüstenhagen (2013), "Whatever the customer wants, the customer gets? Exploring the gap between consumer preferences and default electricity products in Germany", *Energy Policy*, Vol. 53, https://doi.org/10.1016/j.enpol.2012.10.061. [82]

Khan, N. and P. Trivedi (2015), "Gender Differences and Sustainable Consumption Behavior", *British Journal of Marketing Studies*, Vol. 3/3, pp. 29-35, https://www.eajournals.org/wp-content/uploads/Gender-Differences-and-Sustainable-Consumption-Behavior.pdf. [83]

Kovačićek, T. and R. Franić (2019), *The professional status of rural women in the EU*, https://data.europa.eu/doi/10.2861/212719. [46]

London Assembly (n.d.), *Women's Night Safety Charter*, https://www.london.gov.uk/what-we-do/arts-and-culture/24-hour-london/womens-night-safety-charter (accessed on 17 January 2022). [34]

MAPA (2021), *Luis Planas presenta el Plan Estratégico de la PAC, dotado con 47.724 millones de euros hasta 2027, que se enviará mañana a la Comisión Europea*, https://www.mapa.gob.es/es/prensa/ultimas-noticias/luis-planas-presenta-el-plan-estrat%C3%A9gico-de-la-pac-dotado-con-47.724-millones-de-euros-hasta-2027-que-se-enviar%C3%A1-ma%C3%B1ana-a-la-comisi%C3%B3n-europea/tcm:30-584010 (accessed on 18 January 2022). [53]

Mitsios, A. et al. (2019), *Eco-Innovation Observatory - Country Profile 2018-2019: Greece*, https://ec.europa.eu/environment/ecoap/sites/default/files/field/field-country-files/eio_country_profile_2018-2019_greece.pdf. [57]

MoADF (2021), *Εθνικό Μητρώο Αγροτικών Συνεταιρισμών και άλλων συλλογικών φορέων*, http://minagric.gr/index.php/el/for-farmer-2/sillogikes-agrotikes-organoseis (accessed on 20 January 2022). [52]

MoEE (2021), *Circular Economy Action Plan*, https://ypen.gov.gr/wp-content/uploads/2021/12/SXEDIO-DRASHS-KO-FINAL_.pdf. [67]

MoEE (2019), *National Energy and Climate Plan - Greece*, https://ec.europa.eu/energy/sites/ener/files/el_final_necp_main_en.pdf. [12]

MoEE (2014), *National Biodiverisy Strategy & Action Plan*, https://ypen.gov.gr/wp-content/uploads/legacy/Files/Perivallon/Diaxeirisi%20Fysikoy%20Perivallontos/Biopoikilotita/20200323_ethniki_strathgiki_biodiversity.pdf. [91]

Murray, A., K. Skene and K. Haynes (2017), "The Circular Economy: An Interdisciplinary Exploration of the Concept and Application in a Global Context", *Journal of Business Ethics*, Vol. 140/3, https://doi.org/10.1007/s10551-015-2693-2. [69]

Nafilyan, V. (2019), *Gender differences in commute time and pay: A study into the gender gap for pay and commuting time, using data from the Annual Survey of Hours and Earnings*, https://www.ons.gov.uk/employmentandlabourmarket/peopleinwork/earningsandworkinghours/articles/genderdifferencesincommutetimeandpay/2019-09-04. [37]

Nainggolan, D. et al. (2019), "Consumers in a Circular Economy: Economic Analysis of Household Waste Sorting Behaviour", *Ecological Economics*, Vol. 166, p. 106402, https://doi.org/10.1016/j.ecolecon.2019.106402. [87]

NECCA (n.d.), *Natural Environment and Climate Change Agency*, https://necca.gov.gr/ (accessed on 2 February 2022). [95]

Ng, W. and A. Acker (2018), "Understanding Urban Travel Behaviour by Gender for Efficient and Equitable Transport Policies", *International Transport Forum Discussion Papers*, No. 2018/01, OECD Publishing, Paris, https://doi.org/10.1787/eaf64f94-en. [104]

OAED (2021), *Ειδικό πρόγραμμα επιχορήγησης επιχειρήσεων για την απασχόληση 3400 ανέργων, πρώην εργαζομένων στις επιχειρήσεις που επλήγησαν λόγω της απολιγνιτοποίησης στις Περιφέρειες της Δυτικής Μακεδονίας και της Πελοποννήσου*, https://www.oaed.gr/storage/apaskholisi/9ees4691o2-thfo.pdf. [32]

OECD (2022), *Self-employed with employees* (indicator), https://doi.org/10.1787/b7bf59b6-en (accessed on 29 January 2022). [101]

OECD (2022), *Self-employed without employees* (indicator), https://doi.org/10.1787/5d5d0d63-en (accessed on 29 January 2022). [98]

OECD (2021), *Entrepreneurship Policies through a Gender Lens*, OECD Studies on SMEs and Entrepreneurship, OECD Publishing, Paris, https://doi.org/10.1787/71c8f9c9-en. [99]

OECD (2021), *Gender and the Environment: Building Evidence and Policies to Achieve the SDGs*, OECD Publishing, Paris, https://doi.org/10.1787/3d32ca39-en. [2]

OECD (2021), *OECD SME and Entrepreneurship Outlook 2021*, OECD Publishing, Paris, https://doi.org/10.1787/97a5bbfe-en. [100]

OECD (2021), *Policy Framework for gender-sensitive public governance*, https://www.oecd.org/mcm/Policy-Framework-for-Gender-Sensitive-Public-Governance.pdf. [77]

OECD (2021), "Promoting gender equality through public procurement: Challenges and good practices", *OECD Public Governance Policy Papers*, No. 09, OECD Publishing, Paris, https://doi.org/10.1787/5d8f6f76-en. [79]

OECD (2021), "Women in infrastructure: Selected stocktaking of good practices for inclusion of women in infrastructure", *OECD Public Governance Policy Papers*, No. 07, OECD Publishing, Paris, https://doi.org/10.1787/9eab66a8-en. [42]

OECD (2020), *EPOC Survey on integrating gender in environmental policies*. [6]

OECD (2020), *EPOC Survey on integrating gender in environmental policies*, https://one.oecd.org/document/ENV/EPOC(2020)9/en/pdf. [11]

OECD (2020), *Gender and Environmental Statistics. Exploring available Data and Developing New Evidence Contents*, OECD, https://www.oecd.org/environment/brochure-gender-and-environmental-statistics.pdf. [58]

OECD (2020), *Global Forum on Environment: Mainstreaming Gender and Empowering Women for Environmental Sustainability - Key Outcomes*, https://doi.org/ENV/EPOC(2020)7/FINAL. [38]

OECD (2020), *OECD Environmental Performance Reviews: Greece 2020*, OECD Environmental Performance Reviews, OECD Publishing, Paris, https://doi.org/10.1787/cec20289-en. [102]

OECD (2020), "Women at the core of the fight against COVID-19 crisis", *OECD Policy Responses to Coronavirus (COVID-19)*, OECD Publishing, Paris, https://doi.org/10.1787/553a8269-en. [1]

OECD (2019), *EPOC Survey on integrating gender in environmental policies - Chile's response*. [55]

OECD (2019), *Gender, Institutions and Development Database*, https://oe.cd/ds/GIDDB2019 (accessed on 1 December 2021). [44]

OECD (2019), *Measuring the Digital Transformation: A Roadmap for the Future*, OECD Publishing, Paris, https://doi.org/10.1787/9789264311992-en. [108]

OECD (2018), *OECD Toolkit for mainstreaming and implementing gender equality - Implementing the 2015 OECD Gender Recommendation on Gender Equality in Public Life*, https://www.oecd.org/gov/toolkit-for-mainstreaming-and-implementing-gender-equality.pdf. [4]

OECD (2017), *2013 OECD Recommendation of the Council on Gender Equality in Education, Employment and Entrepreneurship*, OECD Publishing, Paris, https://doi.org/10.1787/9789264279391-en. [5]

OECD (2017), *Behavioural Insights and Public Policy: Lessons from Around the World*, OECD Publishing, Paris, https://doi.org/10.1787/9789264270480-en. [106]

OECD (2017), *Getting Infrastructure Right: A framework for better governance*, OECD Publishing, Paris, https://doi.org/10.1787/9789264272453-en. [107]

OECD (2016), *2015 OECD Recommendation of the Council on Gender Equality in Public Life*, OECD Publishing, Paris, https://doi.org/10.1787/9789264252820-en. [3]

OECD (2015), *Going Green: Best Practices for Sustainable Procurement*, https://www.oecd.org/gov/public-procurement/Going_Green_Best_Practices_for_Sustainable_Procurement.pdf. [80]

OECD (2015), *OECD Recommendation of the Council on Public Procurement*, OECD Publishing, https://www.oecd.org/gov/public-procurement/OECD-Recommendation-on-Public-Procurement.pdf. [78]

OECD (n.d.), *RE-CIRCLE: resource efficiency and circular economy*, https://www.oecd.org/environment/waste/recircle.htm (accessed on 12 November 2021). [68]

OECD (n.d.), *Recommendation of the Council on the Governance of Infrastructure*, http://legalinstruments.oecd.org. [43]

OG (2022), *Law 4936/2022 - Εθνικός Κλιματικός Νόμος - Μετάβαση στην κλιματική ουδετερότητα και προσαρμογή στην κλιματική αλλαγή, επείγουσες διατάξεις για την αντιμετώπιση της ενεργειακής κρίσης και την προστασία του περιβάλλοντος*, Official Government Gazette. [13]

OG (2021), *Ministerial Decision ΥΠΕΝ/ΓΔΕ/89335/5599 "Approval of the National Action Plan against Energy Poverty, according to para.1 of art.25 of Law 4342/2015" (OJ B 4447/28.09.2021)*, Offical Government Gazette. [24]

OG (2021), *Έγκριση Σχεδίου Δράσης για τις Πράσινες Δημόσιες Συμβάσεις (JMD 14900/2021)*, Official Government Gazette, http://www.mindev.gov.gr/wp-content/uploads/2021/03/%CE%A6%CE%95%CE%9A466%CE%92_08022021_%CE%91%CE%A0%CE%9F%CE%A6%CE%91%CE%A3%CE%97_%CE%95%CE%93%CE%9A%CE%A1%CE%99%CE%A3%CE%97-%CE%A3%CE%A7%CE%95%CE%94%CE%99%CE%9F%CE%A5-%CE%94%CE%A1%CE%91%CE%A3%CE%97%CE%A3_. [75]

OG (2020), *Law 4685/2020 - Εκσυγχρονισμός περιβαλλοντικής νομοθεσίας, ενσωμάτωση στην ελληνική νομοθεσία των Οδηγιών 2018/844 και 2019/692 του Ευρωπαϊκού Κοινοβουλίου και του Συμβουλίου και λοιπές διατάξεις*, Official Government Gazette.   [93]

OG (2018), *Joint Ministerial Decision 1915/2018 "Amendment of No. 48963/2012 (B 2703) JMD, No. 167563/2013 (B 964) JMD and No. 170225/2014 (B135) MD, which have been issued by authorisation of Law 4014/2011, in compliance with Directive 2014/52*, Official Government Gazette.   [41]

OG (2014), *Ministerial Decision 170225/2014 "Specialisation of the contents of the environment licencing folders for works and activities under Category A of the 1958/2012 Decision of the Minister of Environment, Energy and Climate Change (B 21)...*, Official Government Gazette.   [40]

Ostry, J. et al. (2018), *Economic Gains from Gender Inclusion: New Mechanisms, New Evidence; IMF Staff Discussion Notes No. 18/06; October 9, 2018; by J. D. Ostry, J. Alvarez, R. Espinoza, and C. Papageorgiou.*   [71]

Otro Tiempo Otro Planeta (n.d.), *Cuida el medioambiente, recicla tu aceite*, https://otrotiempo-otroplaneta.org/ (accessed on 15 December 2021).   [73]

Palatnik, R. et al. (2014), "Greening Household Behaviour and Waste", *OECD Environment Working Papers*, No. 76, OECD Publishing, Paris, https://doi.org/10.1787/5jxrclmxnfr8-en.   [105]

Petrova, S. (2017), "Illuminating austerity: Lighting poverty as an agent and signifier of the Greek crisis", *European Urban and Regional Studies*, Vol. 25/4, pp. 360-372, https://doi.org/10.1177/0969776417720250.   [17]

Petrova, S. and N. Simcock (2019), "Gender and energy: domestic inequities reconsidered", *Social & Cultural Geography*, Vol. 22/6, pp. 849-867, https://doi.org/10.1080/14649365.2019.1645200.   [18]

Post, C., N. Rahman and E. Rubow (2011), "Green Governance: Boards of Directors' Composition and Environmental Corporate Social Responsibility", *Business & Society*, Vol. 50/1, pp. 189-223, https://doi.org/10.1177/0007650310394642.   [62]

Robinson, C. (2019), "Energy poverty and gender in England: A spatial perspective", *Geoforum*, Vol. 104, pp. 222-233, https://doi.org/10.1016/j.geoforum.2019.05.001.   [15]

SAAMO West-Vlaanderen (n.d.), *samen uitsluiting aanpakken in West-Vlaanderen*, https://www.saamo.be/west-vlaanderen/ (accessed on 17 January 2022).   [23]

Sachs, C. (2006), "Rural women and the environment.", in *Rural gender relations: issues and case studies*, CABI, Wallingford, https://doi.org/10.1079/9780851990309.0288.   [49]

Samek Lodovici, M. et al. (2012), *The role of women in the green economy-The issue of mobility*, European Union, http://www.europarl.europa.eu/studies.   [35]

SDAM (n.d.), *Το Σχέδιο Δράσης του ΥΠΕΝ για την καταπολέμηση της ενεργειακής φτώχειας πορβλέπει επιπλέον 10% ενίσχυση για τις λιγνιτικές περιοχές*, https://www.sdam.gr/index.php/node/325 (accessed on 10 January 2022).   [25]

STEMReturners (n.d.), *STEM Returners*, https://www.stemreturners.com/the-programme/ (accessed on 17 January 2022).   [66]

Stevenson, G. et al. (2021), *Women and the Net Zero economy: A briefing on changes in garment, agriculture and energy supply chains*, https://assets.publishing.service.gov.uk/government/uploads/system/uploads/attachment_data/file/980198/Guidance3-Women--Net-Zero-Economy-Briefing1.pdf (accessed on 15 January 2022). [31]

Strumskyte, S., S. Ramos Magaña and H. Bendig (2022), "Women's leadership in environmental action", *OECD Environment Working Papers*, No. 193, OECD Publishing, Paris, https://doi.org/10.1787/f0038d22-en. [7]

Tzanne, M. (2022), *Οι big μπιζνες 60 γυναικών στην ηλιακή ενέργεια*. [33]

Tzatzaki, V. (2020), "Recent Developments in Environmental Law in Greece: A Commentary", *International Journal of Environmental Protection and Policy*, Vol. 8/3, p. 66, https://doi.org/10.11648/j.ijepp.20200803.13. [94]

U.S. Department of Energy et al. (n.d.), *The U.S. Clean Energy Education & Empowerment (C3E) Initiative*, https://c3e.org/ (accessed on 17 January 2022). [65]

Umaerus, P., M. Högvall Nordin and G. Lidestav (2019), "Do female forest owners think and act "greener"?", *Forest Policy and Economics*, Vol. 99, pp. 52-58, https://doi.org/10.1016/j.forpol.2017.12.001. [48]

Urban Development Vienna (2013), *Gender Mainstreaming in Urban Planning and Urban Development*, https://www.wien.gv.at/stadtentwicklung/studien/pdf/b008358.pdf (accessed on 4 November 2020). [39]

Urban, J. and M. Ščasný (2012), "Exploring domestic energy-saving: The role of environmental concern and background variables", *Energy Policy*, Vol. 47, pp. 69-80, https://doi.org/10.1016/j.enpol.2012.04.018. [19]

Yaccato, J. and J. Jaeger (2003), *The 80% Minority: Reaching the Real World of Women Consumers*, Viking Canada. [85]

Notes

[1] SDG 6 – Ensure availability and sustainable management of water and sanitation for all; SDG 12 – Ensure sustainable consumption and production patterns; SDG 13 – Take urgent action to combat climate change and its impacts; SDG 14 – Conserve and sustainably use the oceans, seas and marine resources for sustainable development; and SDG 15 – Protect, restore and promote sustainable use of terrestrial ecosystems, sustainably manage forests, combat desertification, and halt and reverse land degradation and halt biodiversity loss.

2 Assessing the integration of gender equality in environmental policies and tools in Greece

This chapter assesses the gender sensitivity of policy actions and tools prioritised under Greece's National Energy and Climate Plan (NECP), National Action Plan against Energy Poverty, Just Transition Development Plan, National Strategy for Climate Change Adaptation, circular economy policy framework, and new biodiversity landscape. It presents interlinkages with gender equality and women's economic empowerment, as well as examples of how other OECD countries integrate the gender-environment nexus into their own policies.

2.1. Assessing the gender-sensitivity of climate and environment-related policies in Greece

The interlinkages between climate change and gender equality are increasingly gaining attention in policy and academic debates. The differentiated impacts of climate change on women and men range from food, water and energy insecurity to being casualties of weather-related disasters (OECD, 2021[1]). These impacts are often linked to deeply-rooted social and economic inequalities that render women and girls more vulnerable to biodiversity loss, ecosystem deterioration and decreasing water resources, especially in regions and areas where their livelihoods depend on the environment (Jerneck, 2018[2]).

Vulnerability and exposure to environmental and climate-related risks involves multiple intersecting factors including income level, location, gender, race, and age (Djoudi et al., 2016[3]). Impacts on social groups vary according to their resilience, ability to cope and adaptive capacity (IPCC, 2014[4]). It is therefore essential to include gender along with other considerations when designing policies to combat climate change and environmental degradation at the national and local levels.

Gender-sensitive environmental and climate policies can also support women's economic empowerment and leadership in related activities. Identifying gender gaps in existing national policies and strategies can help spur further actions for increasing women's participation in economic sectors where their presence is limited.

Initiating a gender-sensitive approach in environmental and climate policy-making requires a comprehensive gender assessment of existing national policies and the effects of their implementation. Currently, available data from Greece on the environmental goods and services (EGSS) sector and sex-disaggregated data on labour force participation in environment-related economic activities does not allow for monitoring employment trends, evaluating policy results, forecasting, or redesigning policies for the transition to a low-carbon economy.[1] Greece is not alone in lacking this type of data: a 2019 OECD survey found that sex-disaggregated and gender-sensitive data related to member countries' environmental policies is limited. In addition, non-homogenous data makes comparing countries difficult. In the same OECD survey, gender-environment data reported by countries ranged from labour force participation in environment-related economic activities, to gender differences in energy or transport use, to health-related data on air pollution and exposure to chemicals and harmful substances (OECD, 2020[5]).

The Greek National Energy and Climate Plan (NECP), endorsed in December 2019, integrates climate objectives and energy planning up to 2030, with a particular focus on energy-related sectors and climate change mitigation and adaptation policies (MoEE, 2019[6]). It serves as an umbrella framework for specialised strategies and action plans that craft in more detail national policy measures planned for the coming years. The NECP's ambitious national targets are in line with the Paris Agreement (OECD, 2020[7]), and are reconfirmed in Greece's recently adopted national Climate Law (Box 2.1).

Box 2.1. Greece's first Climate Law

In May 2022, Greece adopted its first "National Climate Law – Transition to climate neutrality and climate change adaptation" (Law 4936/2022). Setting climate targets in line with the European Climate Law, the law presents policies and measures to guide climate change mitigation and adaptation, and the national process for lignite phase-out, until 2050. It includes a policy framework under which climate change mitigation and adaptation strategies are to be developed at the national and regional levels, as well as a new governance structure comprising an Inter-ministerial Committee on Climate Neutrality, chaired by the Minister of Climate Crisis and Civil Protection, a National Observatory for Climate

---

Change Adaptation, and a Scientific Committee for Climate Change in charge of proposing mitigation and adaptation policies.

In line with the Greek National Energy and Climate Plan (NECP), the legislative framework prioritises actions for specific economic and social activities in sectors such as health, tourism, agriculture, forestry, energy, infrastructure, transport, and biodiversity and ecosystems protection. It includes the development, by 2023, of sectoral carbon budgets for the period 2026-2030 for: i) electricity production (energy and heating); ii) transport; iii) industry; iv) buildings; v) agriculture; vi) waste; and vii) land use, land use change and forestry (LULUCF).[2]

All national agencies and ministries will be required to introduce climate change adaptation and resilience measures in their strategic and operational programming. Under the general guidelines provided, such policy measures and actions should focus on, *inter alia*:

- reducing energy consumption and increasing energy performance in all economic sectors;
- increasing renewable energy systems (RES) coverage, based on best available technologies to avoid negative environmental impact;
- gradual phasing out of fossil fuels and substituting with RES;
- gradual phasing out of natural gas use (and phasing in of bio-methane and green hydrogen), especially in transport and industry;
- promoting electric vehicles, sustainable urban development and use of public transport;
- improving the carbon footprint of buildings and infrastructure in urban and peri-urban areas;
- reducing greenhouse gas emissions from waste management;
- increasing greenhouse gas absorption from natural ecosystems.

Specific references are made to developing green infrastructure, inter-modal transport networks and urban green spaces linked to ecosystem services, well-being and quality of life, as well as to promoting sustainable agriculture, fisheries and food production. It is noted that sustainable urban development should take into consideration environmental, social and economic planning and processes.

Climate change adaptation measures, which will be partly financed through revenues from auctioning EU ETS allowances, include diversifying local economies with a focus on sustainability and creating new jobs in regions undergoing lignite phase-out; financing the national Fair Transition Fund; introducing energy saving measures to reinforce low- and middle-income households; addressing energy poverty; and supporting the provision of services of general economic interest.

Source: (OG, 2022[8]) (EC, n.d.[9]).

Neither the NECP nor the Climate Law include explicit gender considerations. Social considerations within their policy categories focus mainly on vulnerable groups such as low-income households, households affected by the just transition, etc. However, the impacts of many of the proposed measures may not be gender-neutral. They may have differentiated impacts on women and men, and therefore a gender equality perspective should be included in in the design and implementation of these measures.

Table 2.1 and the following sections map gender dimensions that could accompany the social considerations included in the Greek NECP and Climate Law. They take into account intersectional vulnerabilities, gender-differentiated behaviour and preferences, as well as gender inequality in decision making and economic activities.

Table 2.1. Gender dimensions of the Greek National Energy and Climate Plan and Climate Law

Environmental policy category	Social considerations	Gender dimensions
Energy supply security	Access to affordable and secure energy; tackling energy poverty	Women face lower quality of life, female single-parent families at higher risk (intersectionality)
Energy efficiency	Retrofitting buildings; upgrading residential buildings of energy-vulnerable households; promoting sustainable mobility and transport	Women's vulnerability due to energy poverty, women's more sustainable consumption patterns (e.g. women more likely to adopt energy-saving and energy-efficient solutions at home)
Low-carbon economy	Increasing RES share in electricity market; implications for local growth and employment in regions undergoing lignite phase out	Women may be excluded from measures to reduce employment loss and other negative effects in the local economy
Climate change adaptation in sectoral policies (tourism, agriculture, transport)	Sustainable agriculture practices to reduce CO_2 and GHG emissions from the LULUCF sector	Gender-sensitive agriculture policies to increase women's participation in the sector, and to promote more sustainable practices
Spatial planning / Bioclimatic urban design	Revising the city structure and functions to be more sustainable; tackling localised phenomena such as "heat islands"	Support women's sustainable mobility patterns, consider women's needs in city planning
Research & Development (R&D)	Develop and mature technology via STEM education (research centres), start-ups etc.	Advance women's presence in green innovation to support the economy's green transformation
Circular economy	Accelerating circular economy actions to unlock growth potential, with links to small and medium-sized enterprises, social economy and technological innovation	See section 2.3

Source: Authors compilation, based on (MoEE, 2019[6]).

2.2. Providing access to affordable and clean energy

2.2.1. Tackling women's energy poverty

Energy poverty affects women in both developed and developing countries. Its severity and impacts vary according to income level, health and quality of life (OECD, 2021[1]). In developing countries, insufficient access to affordable and clean energy and the time spent gathering biomass fuel negatively effects women's ability to pursue income-generating activities and girls' school attendance. In more advanced economies, such as Greece, energy poverty mostly concerns affordability and efficient energy use. Women in Greece spend more time at home than men, and their energy consumption is mainly attributed to household appliance use. Therefore, women's energy usage depends on household income as well as access. Susceptibility to energy poverty further varies according to socio-spatial differentiations between individuals, households and communities (Robinson, 2019[10]). The Greek NECP acknowledges increased levels of energy poverty as a major challenge, though no reference is made to its gender-differentiated impacts.

Vulnerable communities must often rely on polluting sources of energy. Women and girls, who often spend more time indoors due to household responsibilities, are disproportionately affected by to the adverse health impacts of indoor air pollution. For example, exposure to ambient air pollution is linked to adverse impacts on fertility, pregnancy and even newborns, as per recent evidence that fine particles crossing the placenta lead to foetal exposure (Bové et al., 2019[11]).

Energy poverty is linked to increased overall poverty and lower quality of life, both of which exacerbate tensions within households, which can be a contributing factor to gender-based violence (OECD, 2021[1]). Women in Greece, who traditionally manage family budgets and household energy consumption, faced increased challenges from energy use reduction during the country's economic crisis, including emotional impacts (Petrova, 2017[12]) (Petrova and Simcock, 2019[13]).

At the same time, evidence suggests that women are more responsible users of energy than men. Analysis of selected OECD countries suggests that people with higher environmental concern are more likely to adopt energy-saving and energy-efficiency solutions at home. The same analysis indicates that men show less environmental concern compared to women, even though no correlation was found for energy saving activities (Urban and Ščasný, 2012[14]). A 2015 Canadian study on the relationship between consumers' environmental concerns, carbon footprint and socio-economic status showed that women tend to be more environmentally concerned and engaged in pro-environmental household behaviour. Results also showed that single-parent households, usually led by women, are more likely to have a smaller carbon footprint, due to smaller house size, and limited vehicle ownership and use (Huddart Kennedy, Krahn and Krogman, 2015[15]). In a 2020 study in the United Kingdom, women reported engaging in activities with a higher energy footprint than men, but performing them using less electricity (Grünewald and Diakonova, 2020[16]). A 2021 Swedish study examining expenditure patterns for food, furniture and leisure showed that men spend about 2% more money than women on average, but that the GHG emissions associated with their expenditures is about 16% higher. Men tend to spend more on items such as fuel, while women's spending is concentrated on comparatively lower-emitting products and services such as health care, furnishings and clothes (Carlsson Kanyama, Nässén and Benders, 2021[17]).

Box 2.2. Good practices: Public-private initiative for household energy efficiency in Belgium

The Papillon Project, a joint initiative of Belgian social welfare service *Samenlevingsopbouw West-Vlaanderen* and the Bosch company, enables low-income households to lease, rather than buy, energy-efficient appliances such as dishwashers, dryers and washing machines. Households that would otherwise have to rely on energy-inefficient, second-hand appliances therefore have access to more sustainable options. This type of intervention ameliorates women's household tasks and may also help to reduce feelings of guilt about their ecological footprint.

Source: (SAAMO West-Vlaanderen, n.d.[18]).

The Greek National Action Plan against Energy Poverty, adopted in September 2021, aims at reducing energy poverty levels by 50% in 2025 and by 75% in 2030, compared to 2016 data (OG, 2021[19]). Building upon objectives already included in the NECP, it presents a collection of additional policy measures that support more vulnerable groups.

The Action Plan presents nine actions under three policy categories (Table 2.2). They include subsidies for vulnerable households to install energy-autonomous photovoltaic systems, upgraded energy retrofitting for housing, heating subsidies and electricity bill reduction. For building retrofitting, low-income households are expected to have 75% of the cost subsidised, with the remaining 25% covered through an interest-free loans. The subsidy rate will be higher for households in regions undergoing lignite phase out, reaching 90% (SDAM, n.d.[20]).

Table 2.2. Greek National Action Plan against Energy Poverty

Key policy categories and actions

Consumer protection	Energy efficiency and RES usage	Education and awareness-raising
Providing a preferential electricity supply tariff to protect the affected households from extreme and emergency conditions of energy poverty	Energy upgrade of residential buildings of affected households and promoting the installation of RES stations to meet their energy needs	Informing and educating affected households on how to better manage energy use and fight energy poverty, in the framework of the Energy Efficiency Obligation Regimes 2021-2030
Providing specific quantities of energy products at a preferential price to support affected households' energy consumption through an "energy card"	Provide incentives to install RES systems and energy saving technologies in affected households - Just Transition Areas	Introducing targeted information and education actions to affected households and professionals who are tasked with implementing energy saving actions
Protecting affected households through the adoption and implementation of appropriate regulatory measures (access to universal service, smart meters etc.)	Providing incentives to energy-poor households to take up energy efficiency measures - Energy Efficiency Obligation Regime	
	Revising the framework for "energy communities" to address energy poverty	

Note: Author's table, based on information provided in the Greek National Action Plan against Energy Poverty.
Source: (OG, 2021[19]).

Policies to tackle energy poverty and improve energy efficiency should consider women's role and position within households. Providing women and women-led households with financing opportunities, both to support low-income individuals and families and to promote renewable energy consumption, could serve this purpose. For example, when introducing measures to increase installation of self-generating energy offset systems, priority could be given to households based not only on income but also type of household, dependent members etc. For single-person households, policies aimed at reducing energy poverty could also consider factors such as age, gender and location. Measures such as incentives for intergenerational home sharing, in which expenses could be divided, could also be introduced. Finally, behavioural nudging could further improve energy efficiency in households and encourage families to select renewable energy sources (OECD, 2017[21]). Behavioural nudging further targeted to female consumers could support women in their household decision making. Based on the limited research available, women are more susceptible than men to empathy nudging as an incentive for environmental conservation, and would likely step up their environmentally conscious behaviour if financial incentives and empathy nudging were introduced (Czap et al., 2018[22]).

Box 2.3. Good practices: Tackling women's energy poverty with EmpowerMed

The EU-funded project EmpowerMed aims to tackle energy poverty and improve the health of people in Mediterranean coastal areas. With a special focus on women, the initiative raises public awareness of energy poverty, implements practical solutions to alleviate energy pressures on households, and proposes policy recommendations. It assists more than 10 000 people in Albania, Croatia, France, Italy, Slovenia and Spain through EUR 160 000 investments in sustainable energy and EUR 780 000 of savings.

EmpowerMed collects and validates gender-disaggregated data to enable a better understanding of women's roles in addressing energy poverty. According to an EmpowerMed report, none of the

---

countries examined apply gender-responsive energy policies and strategies. However, Spain's social bonus (electricity discount) has recently added single-parent families as a collective in the access criteria. In Spain the majority of single-parent households are female-led.

Source: (EmpowerMed, n.d.[23]).

An example from Spain demonstrates the importance of ongoing public dialogue on energy conservation. In Madrid, neighbourhood communities come together once a month to discuss energy efficiency, sustainable consumption and green behaviour. An NGO trains community members to become local energy agents and promote energy efficiency within their own community. Women are equally involved in this programme: the project managers consider that women are more successful than men in counselling other women to improve energy efficiency behaviour. Peer-learning has proven to be essential in energy efficiency literacy programmes, in which energy saving solutions are shared by social media, and networking events (Ayuntamiento de Madrd, 2019[24]).

2.2.2. Increasing renewable energy share – Phasing out fossil fuel dependency

Greece has made a national commitment to phasing out fossil fuel dependency by reducing lignite mining and use in its electricity production. In line with the NECP, a Just Transition Development Plan (JTDP) was released in 2020 with a budget of over EUR 5 billion from EU and national resources. The JTDP sets an ambitious roadmap to be completed by 2028, transitioning from coal-intensive economic activities in specific regions (i.e. regions highly dependent on lignite mining and electricity production) to alternative ones based on five development pillars: clean energy; industry and trade; smart agricultural production; sustainable tourism; and technology and education. The JTDP aims to:

- guarantee jobs and create new ones;
- offset the socioeconomic effects of lignite phase-out by maintaining and strengthening the social fabric;
- ensure energy self-sufficiency for regions in transition and the country more broadly, while providing development opportunities for local economies.

Given women's employment patterns and their role in local communities, Greece's just transition is likely to have gender-differentiated effects. The shift from fossil-fuel-intensive to low-carbon economic activities will not only impact (traditionally male) workers in the industries affected, but also local economies. Women may become marginalised if not included in transition planning (Box 2.4). Analysis of the closure of the United Kingdom's coal mines in the 1980s showed that while it initially caused a 90% displacement of male workers, a secondary effect was female manufacturing workers in coal regions being crowded out as men moved into jobs previously occupied by women (Aragón, Rud and Toews, 2018[25]).

Box 2.4. Gender Just Transition – employment opportunities for women

Gender equality in the European Commission's guidelines for just transition programmes

In September 2021, the European Commission released a Working Document to guide member states on issues to consider when developing their territorial just transition plans. Gender implications were identified, together with social exclusion and consequences to livelihoods, as impacts of the transition to climate neutrality on employment.

> The European Commission calls for promoting gender equality in the transition to a climate-neutral economy by ensuring equal opportunities through women's labour market participation and entrepreneurship, and equal pay.
>
> Source: (EC, 2021[26]).

At the 2021 United Nations Climate Change Conference of the Parties (COP26), the United Kingdom presidency presented recommendations for governments to ensure a gender-just transition to net zero. They focus on addressing existing barriers to women's economic empowerment, incentivising business to take part in the gender-just transition, and providing a framework of education and social protection for women (Table 2.3).

Table 2.3. G7 recommendations for a gender just transition to net zero

Address underlying barriers to women's economic empowerment	• Understand the barriers faced by women through improving data collected on women in the workforce and engaging women workers, representatives and communities.
	• Increase women's access to finance and technology and financial and digital literacy.
	• Improve access to education and women's participation in STEM subjects to enable them to access new technologies and new jobs.
	• Strengthen women's land rights.
	• Promote women's leadership and engage and support women's organisations.
Influence and support business	• Promote a gender just transition to net zero, which takes a people-centred approach by including social equity in mandatory climate disclosure, e.g. Taskforce on Climate related Financial Disclosures.
	• Develop women's economic empowerment metrics and frameworks that align with business decision-making approaches and language.
	• Encourage businesses to adopt gender sensitive working practices to overcome barriers to women's participation, including flexible working, childcare support and travel provision.
	• Incentivise businesses to increase women's representation through procurement guidelines and public policies that mandate at least 30% female participation.
	• Partner with businesses to deliver up-skilling programmes for women workers, focusing on technical and managerial skills.
	• Facilitate sectoral collaboration and learning with businesses, workers and communities to identify and promote job substitution, transformation and creation.
	• Support initiatives that measure and incentivise responsible business practices including true cost accounting and socio-economic valuation and corporate benchmarking.
	• Use industrial strategies to provide clear demand signals to businesses for workforce needs.
	• Legislate for decent work and ensure companies pay decent wages, safeguard workers' freedom and protect them from harm.
Provide education and social protection	• Engage in education to support women's participation in STEM subjects.
	• Develop more comprehensive social protection schemes in countries where there is risk of job elimination.
	• Design policies that protect informal workers. Providing women greater agency over their working patterns and supporting higher participation in the labour market.

Source: (Stevenson et al., 2021[27]).

A just transition implies equal employment opportunities for women and men. Job creation in regions affected by the transition to a low-carbon economy should be both inclusive and sustainable. Support could focus on prioritising gender-sensitive and gender-responsive financing and investment opportunities, and on gender-balanced skilling and training programmes. Lack of such support could widen the existing employment gap between men and women, considering the lower engagement level that women start from.

Greece has already begun introducing initiatives to address unemployment in lignite-dependent regions. In 2021, a three-year, EUR 48 million programme was launched to support 3 400 former employees in businesses affected by the coal phase-out process in Western Macedonia and the Peloponnese, the two regions where lignite is mined and used for electricity production. The programme covers 100% of all labour costs for displaced workers in the energy, transport and mining sectors, and 75% for displaced workers in the wholesale and retail trade, catering and tourism sectors. The subsidy rises to 100% for women and long-term unemployed persons over 50 years of age. Employment contract duration varies from 12 to 18 months depending on the sector, with longer subsidies for those directly affected by the just transition process (OAED, 2021[28]).

It should be acknowledged that Greece did reach its 2020 binding target on renewable energy for heating and cooling. The country still strives to meet its electricity and transport targets, however (OECD, 2020[7]). Women's role in renewable energy is not defined in national policies, but the legal framework around "energy communities" – i.e. communities of local actors and citizens who participate in the production, distribution and supply of renewables-based energy (OECD, 2020[7]) – is a step towards increasing women's presence in this market. Additional initiatives should be considered, for example as in the case of Germany, where legislative provisions support the participation of co-operatives in auctions for onshore wind and solar photovoltaics by setting lower tariffs for small developers. This has enabled women-led wind energy co-operatives to become active in the energy transition (OECD, 2021[1]).

Box 2.5. Good practices: Greece's first women-led energy co-operative

WenCoop, the first female-centred social energy co-operative in Greece, aims at empowering women by engaging them in energy-related projects. Supported by the Greek Association of Women Entrepreneurs, it is managed collaboratively by 60 women entrepreneurs, with male participation limited to 5%. Women shareholders come from different entrepreneurial backgrounds, and shares may be divided to allow for access. In addition to generating income, the co-operative covers 100% of members' energy consumption. It may also provide energy, free of charge, to vulnerable groups and single-mother families in the area.

WenCoop is completing the construction of a 1MW photovoltaic park in northern Greece. A second photovoltaic park of equivalent capacity is expected to be completed by early 2023. Additional photovoltaic parks, and an expansion to electric mobility, are under consideration.

Source: (Tzanne, 2022[29]).

2.3. Gender-sensitive climate change adaptation measures

The NECP and the National Strategy for Climate Change Adaptation (NSCCA) constitute Greece's main framework for designing climate change adaptation actions. The NSCCA focusses on economic sectors expected to be highly affected by climate change, i.e. agriculture, forestry, health, tourism, energy, infrastructure and transport, land use and spatial planning, fisheries, mining, water management and insurance. Thirteen Regional Climate Change Adaptation Plans are being finalised. Of these, less than half provide analysis of the expected social impacts of climate change to local populations, and only one makes reference to women (though without specific gender-sensitive analysis). Social impacts anticipated under the regional adaptation plans refer to an ageing population; changes in the local labour market;

cost-related implications of increasing temperatures (and associated rising energy consumption); effects on local populations of rising sea levels in coastal zones; and the need to adjust spatial planning in urban areas to align with changes in the social fabric.

2.3.1. Gender-sensitive sustainable cities

The Greek NECP acknowledges that ameliorating spatial planning and energy management at the local level would lead to containing energy consumption in urban areas, eventually reducing their carbon footprint. It also considers sustainable smart cities which utilise ICT and clean energy as a climate change adaptation measure. Investments in innovative solutions for buildings and vehicles, as well as smart meters and smart networks, are expected to enhance sustainable growth, improve quality of life, and help manage natural resources more sustainably (MoEE, 2019[6]).

Improving city design and public transport use would support both gender equality and women's economic empowerment. Green and blue spaces in cities could help to mitigate climate change impacts such as urban 'heat island' effects and floods. Providing safe access to such spaces is highly valuable for all residents, especially so for women who spend more time in their neighbourhoods. Measures linked to reducing energy consumption and GHG emissions in social infrastructure should be carefully evaluated from a gender perspective, considering that women represent the majority of workers in the health and education sectors.[3] The same applies to lighting in street and public spaces, as insufficient lighting hampers women's feeling of safety at night.

Box 2.6. Good practices: London's Women's Night Safety Charter

Forty-four percent of London residents live within five-minutes' walking distance of a park, yet two times more women than men report that safety concerns are a barrier to walking in a public space.

The Women's Night Safety Charter is part of the Mayor of London's Tackling Violence Against Women and Girls Strategy and the city's commitment to the global UN Women Safe Cities and Safe Spaces initiative. All organisations that operate at night are asked to participate by nominating an organisation champion who actively promotes women's night safety, demonstrating to staff and customers that women's night safety is taken seriously, and encouraging reporting by victims and bystanders as part of their communications campaign. Over 600 organisations, associations and companies (including local businesses) have already signed the London's Women's Night Safety Charter.

Source: (London Assembly, n.d.[30]).

Evidence suggests that women's and men's mobility and travel preferences differ, especially as many women's family, household and professional responsibilities require shorter and multiple trips per day. Women often follow more sustainable mobility patterns than men. They show a stronger preference for public transport use and cycling, though an important concern is the fear of possible sexual harassment and abuse.

Although sex-disaggregated data is limited, evidence from OECD and EU countries indicates that women are more willing than men to reduce their car use, and are more positive towards reducing the environmental impact of travel modes (Samek Lodovici et al., 2012[31]). In Germany for instance, 53% of public transport users are women. The worldwide share of women using public transport is 66% (Diehl and Cerny, 2021[32]). Time spent commuting is a factor in women's employment decisions, indicating that women's economic participation is directly affected by the availability of suitable means of transport

(Nafilyan, 2019[33]). Upgrading modes of transport most used by women could facilitate women's access to the labour market (Ng and Acker, 2018[34]) (OECD, 2021[1]).

Box 2.7. Good practices: Gender mainstreaming in urban planning and public transport

Umea, Sweden

The City of Umea, Sweden monitors women's and men's different use of public space, and has designed its public transport system to minimise city traffic and maximise accessibility. The city integrates a gender perspective in mobility management projects and invests in more sustainable modes of transport. In 2015, 66% of women's daily travel was marked as sustainable in Umea, compared to only 43% of men's. Umea aims to increase men's share of sustainable travel to 55%, which requires, among other measures, that men adopt travel patterns more similar to women's, or alternatively to invest in electric vehicles.

Vienna, Austria

In Vienna, Austria, gender aspects are considered at every stage of urban development. Promoting environmentally friendly means of transport and creating a safe and barrier-free city are envisioned to go hand in hand. Vienna takes into account that women are more often exposed to situations that trigger anxiety in public spaces by implementing adequate design of these spaces and adjoining buildings. Moreover, the city aims at barrier-free accessibility of public transport stops as well as barrier-free station and vehicle design. This is intended to facilitate the lives of persons with caregiving tasks such as carrying shopping bags or pushing prams; allowing them to widen their access and activity range.

Source: (OECD, 2020[35]); (Urban Development Vienna, 2013[36]).

2.3.2. Gender-sensitive environmental impact assessment

Greece's national Climate Law proposes that environmental licencing for works and activities include an assessment of future GHG emissions and climate change impacts, a quantitative analysis and assessment, where possible, of the effects of climate change mitigation and adaptation; and determination of any hindrance to achieving climate neutrality goals. The environmental licencing procedure also encompasses an environmental impact assessment of the local socioeconomic environment, though this is limited to expected demographic changes expected and a short description of local economic activities and employment (OG, 2014[37]). The process also includes a public consultation on works and activities being developed (OG, 2018[38]). Including a gender-based analysis in the environmental licensing process would help identify the effect on women's economic empowerment at the local level. Moreover, raising awareness and encouraging women-led organisations to participate in public consultations would support a more gender-balanced approach.

Better access to sustainable infrastructure (transport, energy, water, housing, social infrastructure etc.) is fundamental for enhancing women's economic empowerment and labour force participation. Guaranteeing a gender lens in the governance framework for infrastructure would provide for more inclusive and sustainable outcomes (OECD, 2021[1]).

According to a 2020 OECD Survey on the Governance of Infrastructure, only 9 out of 31 OECD members explicitly align their long-term national infrastructure plans with inclusion and gender mainstreaming policies. Lack of co-ordination between public authorities responsible for gender equality policies, and line ministries or other governmental bodies in charge of infrastructure, could lead to a disassociated approach to gender-responsive infrastructure investments. Improving co-ordination requires building up institutional capacity as well as gender-disaggregated data collection on infrastructure access and use, which could support introducing a gender lens in all stages of an infrastructure project. This would require, in turn, capital budget adaptation to include social and environmental factors (OECD, 2021[39]).

As an extension order of its existing Framework for Infrastructure Governance (Box 2.8), the OECD has developed a toolkit for mainstreaming gender considerations into the infrastructure life cycle phase (OECD, 2021[39]). The OECD Toolkit for Mainstreaming Gender Considerations into Infrastructure and Capital Budgeting highlights the following steps where OECD members apply tools to incorporate gender mainstreaming:

- Long-term vision for gender-responsive infrastructure;
- Women's voice and agency in infrastructure decision making;
- Gender considerations in project appraisal, selection, risk assessment and design;
- Gender-sensitive infrastructure procurement and delivery;
- Gender angle in monitoring and evaluation.

Box 2.8. The OECD Framework for Infrastructure Governance

The 2017 OECD Framework for the Governance of Infrastructure identifies ten "success factors" to help policy makers improve the management of infrastructure policy, from strategic planning to project delivery. It identifies challenges in infrastructure governance, maps the key dimensions of an effective infrastructure policy system, and presents an overview of current practices in infrastructure governance, which include instruments such as public procurement, budgeting, and integrity frameworks.

In 2020, OECD members endorsed the OECD Recommendation on the Governance of Infrastructure, which allows for more gender-inclusive projects, and ensures gender mainstreaming and direct involvement of women throughout the infrastructure governance cycle. In particular, the Recommendation suggests a whole-of-government approach that emphasises gender, resilience, environmental, regional and social perspectives. It serves as a key tool for responsive and efficient decision making and considers multi-disciplinary objectives such as climate resilience and gender equality policy.

Source: (OECD, 2017[40]); (OECD, n.d.[41]).

2.3.3. Sustainable agriculture and forestry

The Greek NSCCA places particular emphasis on agriculture and forestry as part of the land use, land-use change and forestry (LULUCF) sector contributing to CO_2 and GHG emissions. It also recognises these sectors as being more vulnerable to the impacts of climate change. Attention is given to the need to develop rural development, as well as forestry policies, which could adapt to climate change impact and preserve biodiversity. A special focus is granted to sustainable farming practices, organic farming, and to forest ecosystems' adaptation.

Women's participation in agriculture and forestry is often linked to sustainable agriculture, as women hold traditional local knowledge and have an important role in biodiversity conservation and ecosystem-based management. In developing countries, despite agriculture often being a female-dominated sector, women's role in management and ownership is limited due to legal, financial and other barriers that limit their access to land and non-land assets (OECD, 2021[1]), makes the shift to more sustainable practices more difficult to achieve.

The situation is contrary in OECD countries. Female presence is more limited, yet women do experience secure access to land and non-land assets, formal financial resources, and workplace rights (OECD, 2019[42]). Despite agriculture being a male-dominated sector in almost all OECD countries, it is the sector, among those related to the environment, where women are more present.

The share of women employed in the agriculture sector is high in Greece, with women holding about 40% of jobs compared to the OECD average of 27% (Figure 2.1). This could be explained by high ownership levels of land by women in the country (Gkasouka and Foulidi, 2018[43]). The sector is also characterised by high informality, often associated with supporting family farming-related activities, suggesting that the actual share of women's participation may even be higher. Recent analysis for EU member states ranked Greece third in participation of women workers in informal employment in agriculture, behind Romania and Slovenia (European Parliament et al., 2019[44]). However, in many countries, including EU member states, women's land work in rural areas is considered part of their daily household responsibilities so is not recorded in statistics nor linked to social security benefits and public financing opportunities. Women also take on seasonal and part-time agricultural jobs which may not be recorded in data collection (EIGE, n.d.[45]).

The same applies to forestry, where men's participation is six times higher than women's on average in OECD countries. In Greece the difference is much smaller, with about one woman for every three men in the sector, though the economic activity is also limited (Figure 2.1).

Evidence suggests that men and women set different priorities on forest management. A study in Sweden shows that men forest owners value as a main objective the increase in timber production, while women value the preservation of forests, plants, animals and cultural environment (Umaerus, Högvall Nordin and Lidestav, 2019[46]).

Guaranteeing gender sensitivity in agriculture and forestry policies could increase women's participation in the sector while also supporting a shift towards sustainable and organic farming. Evidence indicates that women tend to adopt sustainable organic farming practices in some OECD countries (Sachs, 2006[47]) (Dinis et al., 2015[48]) and apply for agri-environmental government subsidies (e.g. in Italy) (Chiappini and De Rosa, 2011[49]).

Figure 2.1. Employment in environment-related economic activities, by gender

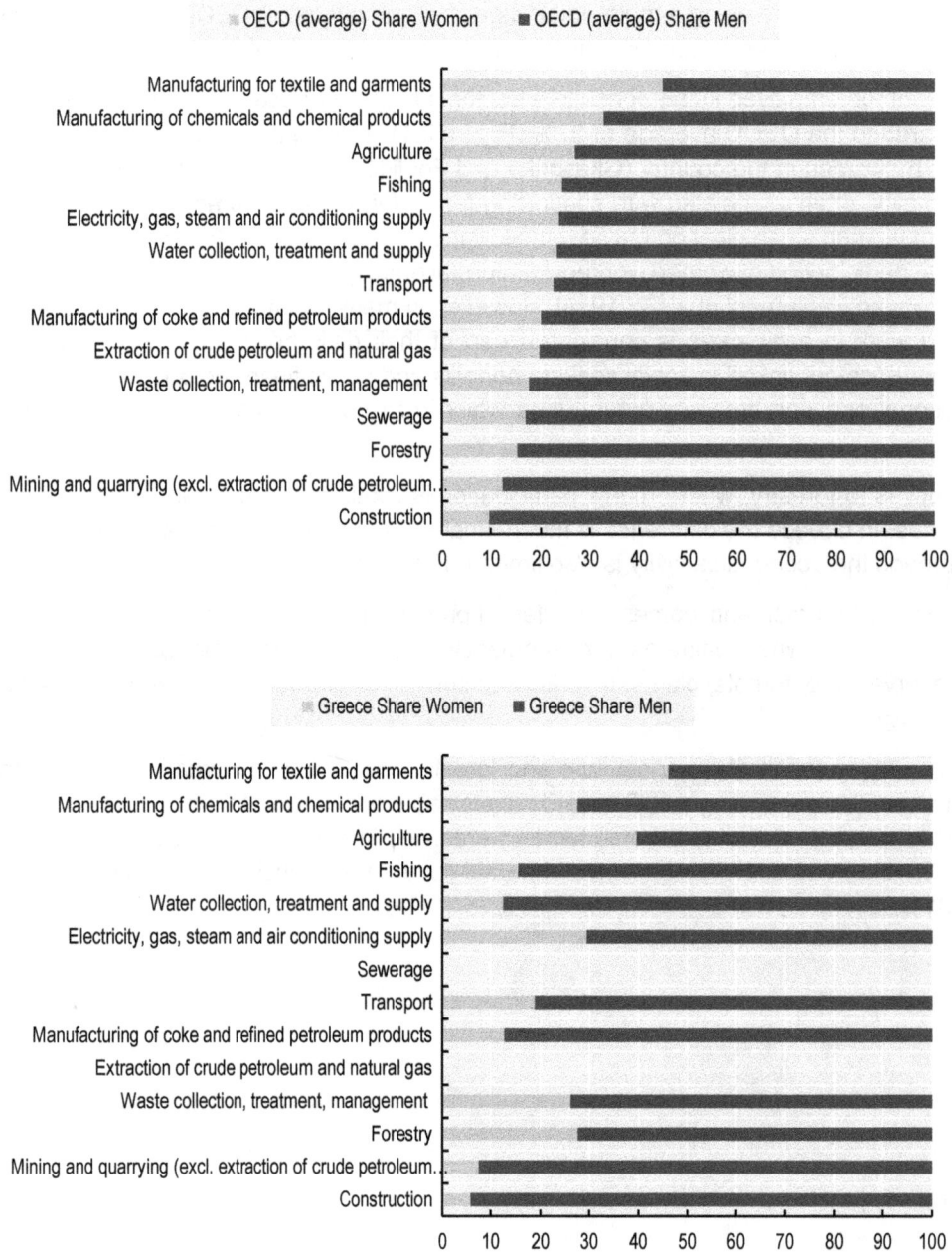

Note: 2020 data, expect for UK (2019). Average for OECD does not include data for Australia, Canada, Chile, Colombia, Israel, Japan, Korea and New Zealand. Data used under economic activity classification ISIC-Rev.4 (2-digit level).
Source: ILOSTAT.

Gender-sensitive agriculture and forestry policies could also help to maintain a younger and well-educated population in rural areas (European Parliament et al., 2019[44]). A 2017 survey of women farmers commissioned by the Greek General Secretariat for Gender Equality indicated that 71% of respondents were aware of new farming processes (organic farming, environmentally-friendly crops) even if they did not practice them, 45% expressed an interest, and 54% expected such farming to attract young women back to rural areas. The same study identified a need for targeted government programmes to enhance women farmers occupation with organic farming, as well as a need to revise tax policies, social charges and pension schemes, which would acknowledge women's different sources of income (for example from participation in women-led farmers co-operatives in parallel to their own agricultural activity). Finally, it encouraged the participation of women farmers in decision-making processes at the local and national level (Gkasouka and Foulidi, 2018[43]).

National legislation also exists on setting up Women-led Farmers' Co-operatives, in an attempt to support women's engagement in agricultural activities and leadership. The results of such initiative are still to be shown, yet advancing women's activity would require some measures of positive discrimination. So far, only 3% of registered co-operatives and associations are women-led, focusing in agro-tourism and handcrafting activities (MoADF, 2021[50]). Financial and other incentives could be put into place to advance such co-operatives, with a focus on sustainable activities, in comparison to other farmers' co-operatives.

Spain's proposed Common Agricultural Policy (CAP) Strategic Plan 2023-2027 includes some gender elements. The plan highlights reducing the gender gap and supporting generational replacement, notably as two thirds of active farmers are expected to retire in the next decade. To counterbalance the negative effects to agricultural labour, there will be premiums of up to 15% of aid to incorporate young farmers and livestock farmers (MAPA, 2021[51]). Ireland is also introducing policies to support women's participation in farming; which include targeted grant aid of 60% to women up to 55 years of age, in comparison to men who receive 40%; as well as increasing women's knowledge and adoption of innovative farming approaches through a Knowledge Transfer tillage scheme and their participation at the European Innovation Partnerships (DoAFM, 2021[52]). Chile has introduced a training programme for rural women, under the auspices of the national Institute for Agricultural Development (INDAP) and the Foundation for the Promotion and Development of Women (PRODEMU). The programme, which has a duration of three years, considers women's participation in the productive promotion of forestry, agro-industrial activities, rural tourism or handicrafts, with a focus on environmental sustainability (OECD, 2019[53]).

In La Rioja, Spain, a draft of the Law on Agriculture and Livestock was recently presented. It introduces the principle of positive discrimination towards young people and women in public administration actions. Such measure, favouring the owners of agricultural holdings or those in the process of gaining access to the ownership of holdings, is expected to provide motivation to youth and women to more actively get engaged with agricultural production (Agroinformacion, 2022[54]).

No specialised programmes addressing women's engagement in the forestry sector are currently under consultation in Greece. The Ministry of Environment and Energy is in discussions for additional staff in charge of developing forest maps for the national forest registry, to be financed through general interest programming (services accessible to the public). Prioritisation is given to long-term unemployed and vulnerable groups with technical qualifications. The programme will also provide training to those participating. However, no gender considerations are so far included in this programme, while some prerequisites for participation (such as limitation to only one person per household to participate in the call) could discourage qualified women to apply.

2.4. Increasing women's participation in environment-related innovation

The Greek NECP sets a target of doubling R&D budget allocations for energy and environment between 2017 and 2030. This is expected to improve Greece's competitiveness by enhancing energy efficiency and reducing energy costs; to increase the energy sector's value added through creating or maintaining 60 000 labour positions; and to tackle challenges arising from lignite phase-out (MoEE, 2019[6]). It is unclear how new jobs will link to R&D budget allocations or if they will be "green".

Greece's R&D budget allocations for energy and the environment are highly dependent on EU funding and critically lower than the OECD average, despite an upward trend from 2008 to 2017 (OECD, 2020[7]). In

2017 and 2018, there was a decrease in R&D funding for energy and environment as a percentage of the government's total R&D budget (Figure 2.2).

Figure 2.2. Greek government R&D budgets for energy and the environment, 2008-18

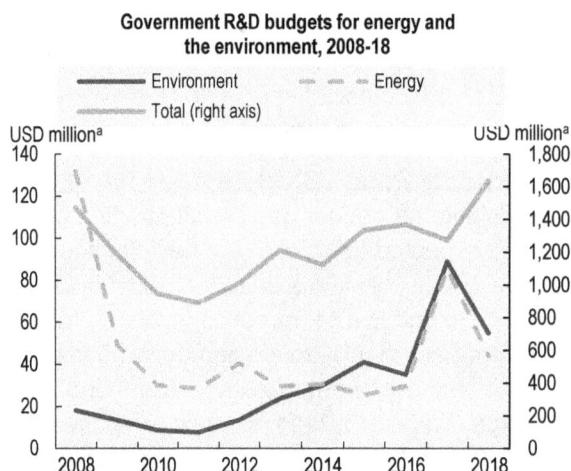

Note: a) At 2010 prices and purchasing power parities.
Source: (OECD, 2020[7]).

Greece is performing modestly in innovation compared to other EU countries. Structural limitations such as a fragmented R&D framework, limited access to finance, and weak linkages between science and business exist (OECD, 2020[7]). The characteristics of Greek businesses (mainly micro- and small firms with low productivity levels and low value added (OECD, 2021[55])) limit their capacity to invest and capitalise benefits from innovation. This trend also applies to eco-innovation, despite Greece's promotion of innovation in industrial and municipal waste management; anti-pollution technologies and industrial symbiosis; utilisation of the marine environment's wealth; and the participation of business in efforts to increase resource efficiency and biodiversity (Mitsios et al., 2019[56]).

Women's participation in sciences and innovation could both enrich environmental outcomes and help overturn deep-rooted perceptions and social norms regarding their role. However, in education women show a low take-up of STEM (science, technology, engineering and mathematics) subjects when compared to men, which could potentially translate into a lower representation in research and development, and therefore green innovation (OECD, 2021[1]). More resources and actions are needed to promote programmes that increase the uptake of scientific research and innovation by women, and to tackle the barriers to their participation in STEM education.

Comparing country data, women's participation in developing green inventions (environmental technologies) in Greece is 13%, higher than the OECD average of 11%. The same does not apply to all technologies, despite the fact women inventors almost doubled between 1990-02 and 2015-17 (Figure 2.3). In general, there is no uniformity between countries when comparing the level of women's participation in environmental or other technologies, the level of green innovation in the country's economic activity and the level of gender equality in policy making, which implies that for each country there are various factors that should be considered coherently to achieve greater women's inclusion in green technologies, and the green economy more widely.

Figure 2.3. Share of women inventors by country

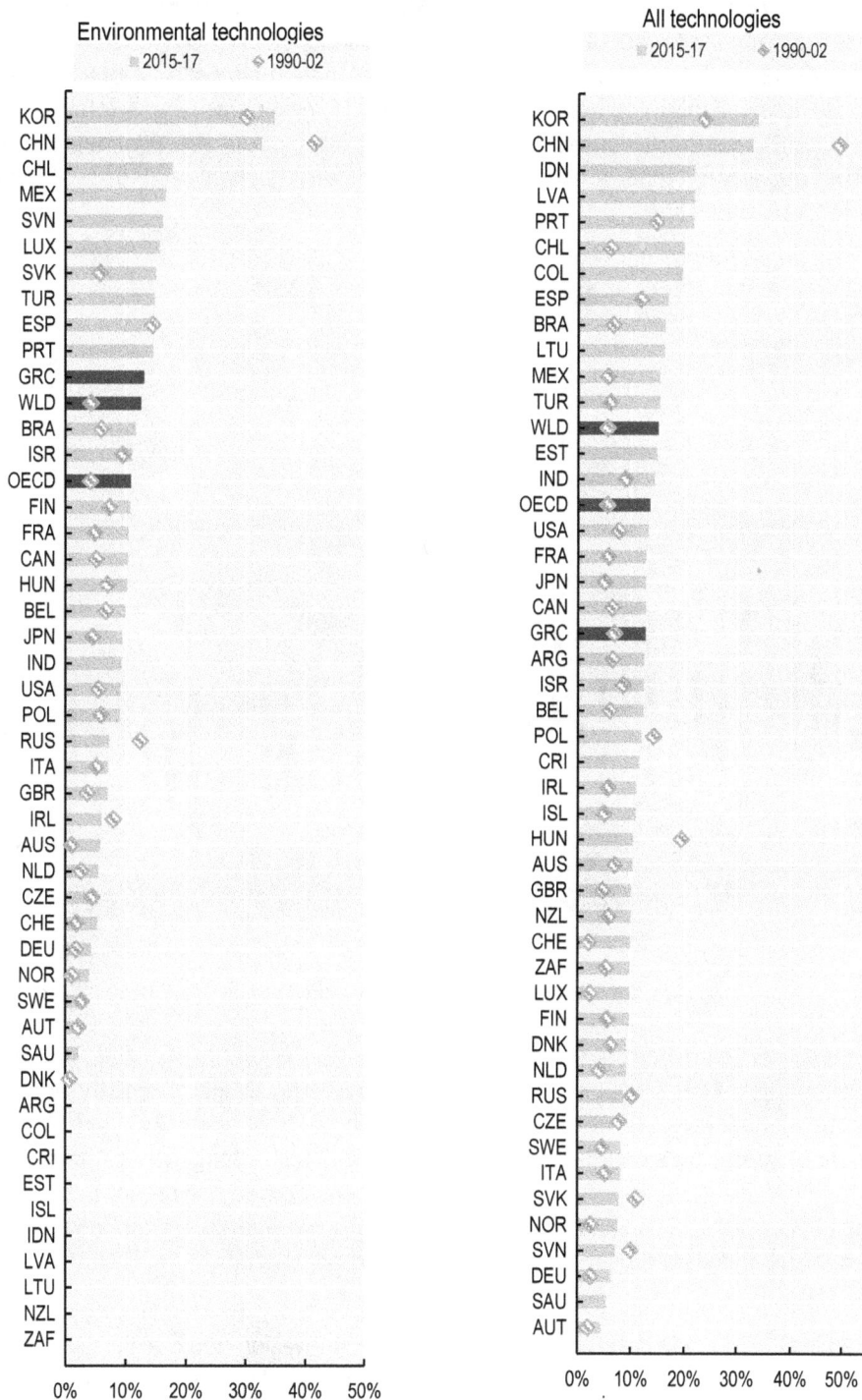

Environmental technologies
■ 2015-17   ◇ 1990-02

KOR, CHN, CHL, MEX, SVN, LUX, SVK, TUR, ESP, PRT, GRC, WLD, BRA, ISR, OECD, FIN, FRA, CAN, HUN, BEL, JPN, IND, USA, POL, RUS, ITA, GBR, IRL, AUS, NLD, CZE, CHE, DEU, NOR, SWE, AUT, SAU, DNK, ARG, COL, CRI, EST, ISL, IDN, LVA, LTU, NZL, ZAF

0% 10% 20% 30% 40% 50%

All technologies
■ 2015-17   ◇ 1990-02

KOR, CHN, IDN, LVA, PRT, CHL, COL, ESP, BRA, LTU, MEX, TUR, WLD, EST, IND, OECD, USA, FRA, JPN, CAN, GRC, ARG, ISR, BEL, POL, CRI, IRL, ISL, HUN, AUS, GBR, NZL, CHE, ZAF, LUX, FIN, DNK, NLD, RUS, CZE, SWE, ITA, SVK, NOR, SVN, DEU, SAU, AUT

0% 10% 20% 30% 40% 50%

Note: Values based on less than 10 high-value inventions (claimed priorities) are not shown. Countries not meeting this threshold are shown as data not available (n/a).

Source: OECD (2020), OECD Environment Statistics (database); OECD calculations based on extractions from EPO (2019) and using dictionaries from Lax Martínez et al. (2016) and search strategies developed by OECD.

Women are less present in technical subjects in education and research, such as physics and digital technology (computer science), despite progress in their participation in specific scientific subjects. On average, in natural sciences, engineering and ICTs (NSE & ICT) women comprise over 7% of all tertiary graduates, with men accounting for about 16%. Greece is marking a higher presence of women graduates in NSE & ICT, with the share of women at over 11% and that of men at almost 17% of all tertiary graduates. Overall, Greece maintains a high percentage of NSE & ICT graduates, over total graduates, when compared to other OECD countries (Figure 2.4). Yet, women's labour market participation in STEM-related fields remains low, suggesting that gender stereotypes, cultural beliefs and implicit biases hamper women's access to these professions.

Figure 2.4. Tertiary graduates in natural sciences, engineering and ICTs (NSE & ICT), by gender, 2016

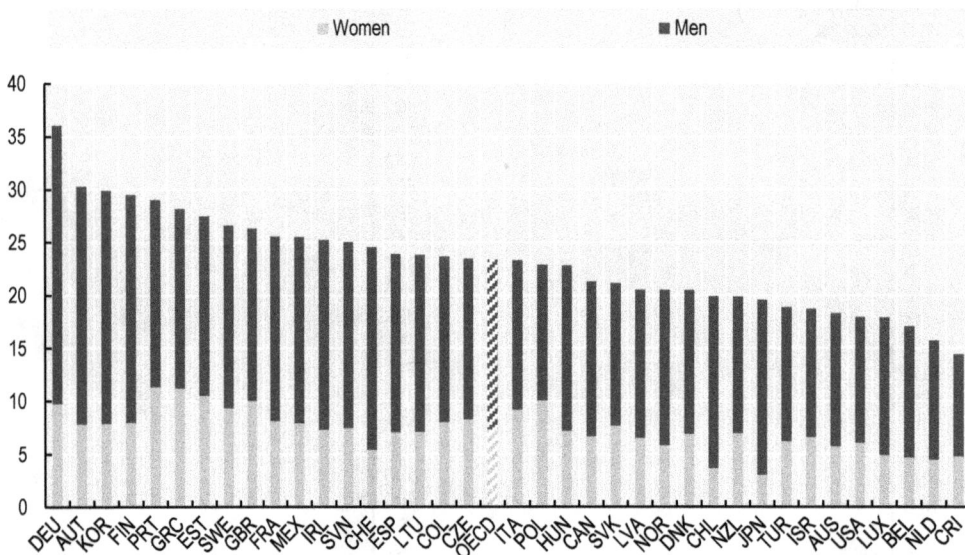

Source: (OECD, 2019[57]).

In parallel, there seems to be an increasing participation of women inventors in certain patenting activities, though their overall participation remains relatively low on average. While chemistry and health-related technologies had the highest levels of women's participation in 2016, at about 24% and 20% respectively, environmental technologies only exceeded 12%. Thus, there is still a long way to go to achieve better participation of women in developing green technologies. Where women are present, it tends to be in so-called new domains such as solar photovoltaic and climate change adaptation technologies. Women are less present in transport and wind power technologies, where engineering – i.e. STEM-based – skills are required (OECD, 2020[58]).

Supporting women in STEM studies and green research and innovation could also have positive impacts towards increasing women's presence in traditionally male-dominated sectors, as well as those economic activities that are more "green". For example, an International Renewable Energy Agency's (IRENA) survey indicated a larger concentration of women in the renewable energy sector (32%) than the oil and gas industry (22%). This could imply a larger interest for women in environmental sustainability, nonetheless, women are mainly present in the administrative and non-technical positions (35%) rather than those that are STEM-related (28%) (IRENA, 2019[59]). Initiatives to support girls' education and women's careers linked to STEM would require a holistic approach targeting not only the interested parties, but also educators, career counsellors, and research agencies, in an attempt to break existing barriers.

Box 2.9. Good practices: Australia's strategy for women in STEM

The Australian Government's strategy for women in science, technology, engineering and mathematics (STEM) aims to increase gender equity in STEM education and careers. They envision a society that provides equal opportunity for people of all genders to learn, work and engage in STEM. The government leads and supports action in three areas: (i) enabling STEM potential through education, (ii) supporting women in STEM careers, and (iii) making women in STEM visible.

In order to support action on gender equity, the government is focusing on long-term strategic interventions, for instance through the Women in STEM and Entrepreneurship (WISE) grants programme. Announced under the National Innovation and Science Agenda (NISA), the WISE programme has already provided AUS 8 million to support 46 projects and will continue to provide up to AUS 1 million per year to support targeted STEM gender equity initiatives.

To enable STEM potential through education, the Australian government has committed over AUS 500,000 to the development of a Girls in STEM Toolkit, which was delivered in August 2019. The Toolkit aims at educating girls, as well as parents, teachers, career counsellors and other influencers, on opportunities in STEM. Another AUS 25 million over ten years were invested to support the greater participation of Indigenous girls in STEM.

Furthermore, the Australian government provided AUS 2 million over 3 years to support the expansion of the Science in Australia Gender equity (SAGE) pilot that includes 44 Australian universities, medical research institutes and research agencies. The pilot was found to have a positive impact and demonstrated the potential for transformational change.

Source: (DISER, n.d.[60]).

Moreover, women's empowerment and leadership in the energy sector may play a catalytic role in ensuring access to affordable, reliable, sustainable and modern energy services for all. Evidence suggests that private firms with more women in their governing boards and senior management are more likely to take sustainable initiatives compared to those with no gender diversity (Hossain et al., 2017[61]) (Post, Rahman and Rubow, 2011[62]). At the same time, energy continues to be one of the sectors were women are less present in senior official and management positions when compared to others in government and business (either corporate or small enterprises) (IEA, 2020[63]). Initiatives such as the C3E, supported by the International Energy Agency (IEA), could be adapted to Greece and, with the engagement of local actors, support women's presence in the renewable energy workforce (Box 2.10).

Box 2.10. Good practices: Advancing women's participation and leadership in the clean energy sector

The Clean Energy Education and Empowerment (C3E) initiative was launched at the Clean Energy Ministerial in 2010. Supported by the International Energy Agency, C3E focuses on enabling greater diversity in the clean energy professions. By bringing together public administration, private sector and academia, the initiative aims at identifying best practices and enabling data and experience sharing on career development. The C3E Technology Collaboration Programme is developing indicators to monitor the progress of women's participation in the clean energy sector workforce.

C3E in the United States

The United States C3E Initiative was launched in 2010 and is led by the United States Energy Department in collaboration with the MIT Energy Initiative, Stanford's Precourt Institute for Energy and Texas A&M Institute. The initiative includes the C3E awards that are acknowledging mid-career women who have an outstanding leadership and accomplishments in clean energy. Furthermore, it engages in promoting concrete, visible and measurable actions that encourage women's participation and leadership in the energy sector.

The United States Energy Department is committed to advancing women's participation and leadership in the energy workforce, and in furthering STEM education by working in partnership with stakeholders to inspire girls and women to go into science, technology, engineering, and math careers and seeking to remove barriers to participation in STEM.

Source: (C3E International and IEA, 2019[64]) (U.S. Department of Energy et al., n.d.[65]).

Any efforts would also require support in breaking possible access barriers, which not only limit women's initial entry to STEM-related and green occupations, but also their advancement (for a definition of green jobs/occupations see Box 3.2). The United Kingdom Institute of Marine Engineering, Science and Technology, together with the Women's Engineering Society, have introduced the STEM Returners project, which offers paid short-term work placement for women and men restarting their professional career. According to the project's findings, over half of those participating in the project with the aim to return to employment are women, when the number of women already in marine engineering, science and technology in the UK reaches only 8% (STEMReturners, n.d.[66]).

2.5. Women's role in the circular economy

Greece released a two-year national Circular Economy Action Plan (CEAP) in 2021, aiming to better align the national framework to the European Commission's European Green Deal and Circular Economy Action Plan. The 2021-2023 Action Plan encompasses 59 actions, grouped under the following axis: (i) sustainable production and industrial policy; (ii) sustainable consumption; (iii) less waste with higher value; and (iv) horizontal actions, i.e. on governance and monitoring, to cover all above; and (v) specialised actions for priority basic products (MoEE, 2021[67]).

In parallel, several legislative and other initiatives have been adopted in the period 2019-2021, including among others a new legal framework on waste management, an action plan for green public procurement, initiatives to reduce food waste, and financial (dis-)incentives based on pay-as-you-throw principle and promoting products' eco-design. These initiatives are also depicted in the CEAP, in line as well with the NECP priorities (MoEE, 2021[67]).

Business models that are more resource efficient and promote the reduce-recycle-reuse triptych, are core to the transition towards a circular economy. A circular economy in its turn is expected to strengthen growth prospects, increase the competitiveness of domestic firms and create jobs in innovative sectors (OECD, n.d.[68]). When the circular economy is supported by advancements in the Information and Communications Technology (ICT) sector and digitalisation, it can contribute to both resource productivity growth and reduction in negative environmental externalities associated with resource lifestyle. Beyond the environmental and business aspects of circularity, a circular economy should also consider social implications and opportunities, so as to guarantee inter- and intra-generational equality in the long-run (Murray, Skene and Haynes, 2017[69]). One of the social implications to be considered should be gender equality.

Engaging women in the circular economy - through supporting their integration in green jobs (see Box 3.2), awareness-raising on sustainable consumption and encouraging participation in leadership and managerial roles - is indispensable to create good circular systems. A move towards a more circular economy can be designed to encourage gender equality. As women are more often segregated into low pay, low security and limited social mobility jobs, the rise of green jobs as part of the circular economy movement offers an opportunity to empower women (ILO, 2015[70]). Integrating gender considerations in a circular economy framework may also lead to an increase in women's participation in the economic activity. Based on 2020 data, women in Greece occupy about 26% of positions in waste collection, treatment and supply, higher than the OECD average which is at 18% (Figure 2.1).

Even though no gender analysis was undertaken when developing the Greek CEAP, some of the actions proposed could have a direct impact on gender equality and women's economic empowerment (Table 2.4).

Table 2.4. Greek Circular Economy Action Plan's gender considerations

Gender considerations	Actions in CEAP
Boost women's participation in green labour market / Support women's inclusion in green entrepreneurship - Provide positive discrimination to achieve gender equality in green economic sectors	Incentives for the design and production of products that support circular economy models and the establishment of an SME support mechanism
	Integration of criteria for sustainable production in extended producer responsibility programmes
	Creation, organisation and licensing of new Alternative Management Systems (ALS) (textiles, vehicle spare parts, photovoltaic panels, wind turbines, pesticide packaging, expired medicines, mattresses, furniture, fishing gear, tobacco products)
	Establish a financing programme for constructing new and modernising existing infrastructure for source screening, recycling and waste recovery to achieve the objectives of the new national waste management plan
	Institutionalisation of mandatory criteria for green public procurement and related objectives
	Formulation of a special action plan for tourism and a special action plan for blue development
Feminising green consumption patterns	Informing and educating consumers on sustainable consumption issues
	Institutionalisation of an integrated framework of financial incentives and disincentives to reduce municipal waste production
	Formulation of a special action plan to reduce food waste
Support women's engagement with green innovation	Joint state aid action "Research-Create-Innovate"
	Actions to promote the creation of a non-toxic environment
Enhance women's representation and leadership in environment-related sectors	Creating a circular economy coordinating body
	Establishing a national circular economy observatory
	Setting a national initiative "Circular Alliance for Greece" and signing voluntary agreements with stakeholders

Source: Author's graph, based on information provided in the Greek Circular Economy Action Plan (MoEE, 2021[67])

2.5.1. Supporting women's inclusion in green entrepreneurship and sustainable production

Recent OECD analysis on the labour implications of the transition to a resource efficient and circular economy shows that there is an expected increase in green jobs by 2040, as in the secondary-based metal production and recycling sectors (Chateau and Mavroeidi, 2020[71]). At the same time, narrowing the gap between men and women in labour force participation, is expected to bring larger than expected economic gains, due to the positive impact of gender inclusion on growth, and the welfare gains from removing social and other barriers. This is even more so the case in sectors where there is limited women's participation, as for example the environment-related sectors and circular economy sectors (Ostry et al., 2018[72]).

Introducing green growth policies and moving towards a green transition through climate and energy policies are expected to have higher labour implications in labour-intensive sectors, such as mining and quarrying, electricity, chemicals and food products (Chateau, Bibas and Lanzi, 2018[73]). A shift to a green economy is likely to be accompanied by a declining demand for dangerous occupations, as for example in mining, even though health and other risks may also be associated to green occupations, such as in construction or recycling (Botta, 2019[74]).

Nevertheless, a shift to jobs in the low-carbon economy would also require developing a set of green skills (see Section 3.2.1). Analysis shows that these skills would probably be a combination of "traditional" skills (e.g. autonomy and communication) and generic green skills (e.g. reducing waste), meaning that up-skilling, rather than re-skilling, may be more appropriate for workers in traditional "brown" sectors (e.g. emission intensive sector such as heavy industries). Yet, considering the limited female participation in traditional "brown" sectors which may now be shifting to net-zero, a different, more targeted, approach may be required for women willing to enter the green job market. This should also be topped up with initiatives to attract women towards STEM education, and to promote vocational training and job opportunities in green sectors to women, since these may require a combination of technical and physical skills (Botta, 2019[74]).

In parallel, the shift to more circular economic models may also have an effect to sectors such as textile and garment manufacturing, where women in Greece hold the highest participation rate when compared to other environment-related sectors (Figure 2.1); or to other sectors that will become more digitalised, and which again will require a different set of skills.

Women could also play a catalytic role in shifting companies' corporate decisions to more sustainable options, as their presence in corporate boards and senior-management positions can improve companies' environmental performance (Strumskyte, Ramos Magaña and Bendig, 2022[75]). Evidence shows that company corporate boards with at least three female members tend to take more responsible decisions on issues linked to pollution prevention, emissions reduction, use of recycled materials in production, and use of renewable energy. Such companies also show a higher commitment to environment-related reporting (Post, Rahman and Rubow, 2011[62]). A more equitable representation of women in decision-making positions in the private sector may indicate a shift to more circular initiatives and eventually a shift to more circular business models.

Entrepreneurship is often seen by women as a way out of limitations that are linked to existing barriers in the labour market or to their multiple responsibilities (household, care responsibilities, professional etc.). Women show a preference to self-employment as it offers more flexible working hours, and it also allows them to avoid the "glass ceiling". Nevertheless, women face other barriers when entering self-employment and entrepreneurship, such as an unsupportive culture, a fear of lack of entrepreneurial skills, limited access to finance, more condensed and usually less effective entrepreneurial networks, and often conflicting family and tax policies (OECD, 2021[76]). It is worth noting that Greece scores the highest levels of self-employed men among OECD countries, either with or without employees. Self-employed women are also predominantly own-account workers (i.e. work for and by themselves), however Greece scores the highest among OECD countries in the category self-employed with employees (OECD, 2022[77]); (OECD, 2022[78]). Despite their large presence in self-employment – and therefore entrepreneurship - 66% of Greek women entrepreneurs report that "fear of failure" is a barrier to business creation, when the OECD average is around 50%, indicating the significant need to overcome the existing unsupportive culture, and other barriers (OECD, 2021[76]).

These barriers apply also to green entrepreneurship. Advancing women's engagement into green entrepreneurship, that could support a circular economy, would require tailored initiatives around finance, skills and support. These could be supporting green entrepreneurship education and green skills, including skills necessary for circular business models; facilitating access to financial resources, accompanied also by courses in financial literacy; and setting up networking and mentoring programmes for women in green entrepreneurship (Strumskyte, Ramos Magaña and Bendig, 2022[75]).

Box 2.11. Good practices: The FIT initiative

The "Financial literacy and new business models to boost women entrepreneurship possibilities" (FIT) initiative advocates for empowering women's entrepreneurial activities, using circular economy business models. A team of six organisations from Greece, Italy, Lithuania, Malta, Poland, and Spain aims at preparing and testing a learning and coaching programme specifically designed to support women entrepreneurs in starting or reshaping their business, using circular economy business models, and appropriate financial planning. The programme aims at supporting women entrepreneurs in:

- Learning about new business models and contributing to the green economy;
- Increasing their financial literacy and sound financial and strategic management skills;
- Developing managerial and leadership skills; and
- Increasing networking and mentoring opportunities.

Source: (FIT, n.d.[79]).

Directly linked to the Greek CEAP, it is worth exploring specialised training programmes for green skills and financial literacy targeted to women and financial incentives for women-owned green businesses related to circular economy activities or business models. Acknowledging women's high presence in the services sector, incentives to promote product service system models - where services rather than products are marketed - could potentially benefit women more if accompanied with other measures overcoming structural and other barriers mentioned above.

Socially sensitive and innovative projects aimed at providing women's economic security do exist. In Spain, the women-led Otro Tiempo Otro Planeta initiative provides women at risk of social exclusion or victims of gender-based violence with an opportunity to actively participate in an economic activity. Women collect and transport used cooking oil and recycle it to alleviate risks of polluting waste and of maintaining municipal waste infrastructure. The initiative installs containers for used cooking oil in common spaces in neighbourhoods, which are then collected and replaced with clean ones. In 2015, over 30 000 litters of biodiesels was produced from the collected cooking oil. The initiative follows the principle of work-life balance by establishing flexible working hours for its workers, teleworking, assistance for workers with dependent family members, training and income generation, and transferable working hours to accommodate family needs (Otro Tiempo Otro Planeta, n.d.[80]).

2.5.2. Gender-sensitive green public procurement

Greece has been committed to green public procurement (GPP) since 2010, excluding suppliers that do not comply with environmental regulations and standards (OECD, 2020[7]). In February 2021, a three-year national Action Plan for Green Public Procurement (APGPP) was introduced to align the national framework with EU legislation and guidelines on introducing environmental considerations and circularity in public procurement. Special focus is given to five product categories: paper, cleaning products, IT equipment, air conditioning and lighting. The Action Plan is aligned with European Commission methodology (EC, 2016[81]), whereby public procurement needs to take into consideration the budgetary, environmental and market impacts of each tender. Annual quantitative targets are set for the procurement of certain products and services under green criteria (eco-labelling, certification, technical requirements and standards etc.) (OG, 2021[82]). These are to be gradually implemented by public authorities (national, regional and local). The Action Plan is supported by capacity building exercises, where training is offered to both public officials and suppliers willing to participate in the procurement procedures (EC, 2021[83]). Such training envisions to inform and raise awareness on both the environmental and social benefits from procuring products and services that are friendly to the environment (OG, 2021[82]).

Gender mainstreaming in public policies could bring gender inequalities to the forefront and assist policy makers in taking more informed and fair decisions. Gender-sensitive public governance can contribute to identifying gender-related integrity breaches; improving awareness of existing gender inequalities; promoting inclusiveness, participation and diversity; and supporting access to justice. Public procurement could be a strategic lever to promote gender equality, by lifting embedded biases and gender stereotypes in the public procurement policy framework. Such an approach could both boost women's economic empowerment, through their active participation in procurement procedures, and guarantee a more gender-sensitive and gender-responsive approach to public purchases (OECD, 2021[84]).

Adopting a sustainability approach to public procurement could potentially stimulate a better environmental and social performance of products and services purchased. Reinforcing the Greek Action Plan on Green Public Procurement with gender-responsive initiatives, could help achieve a more sustainable and just approach to procurement processes. Such initiatives could include:

- Expanding capacity building exercises to cover both environmental and gender equality standards;
- Collecting data on women-led enterprises, as well as enterprises which apply gender equality standards, as well as on enterprises applying green standards and circular business models;
- Evaluating the gender- and environmental impact of bids, through consultation with other public authorities and civil society which could present knowledge to better frame the public procurement process in a more gender-neutral and environmentally sustainable manner.

The OECD Recommendation of the Council on Public Procurement recognises that adhering countries may use the public procurement system to pursue secondary policy objectives, such as gender equality and/or environment, however this should be done in a balanced way against the primary procurement objective (OECD, 2015[85]). Therefore, complementarities and trade-offs between the different objectives should be identified and impact measured. OECD analysis has also highlighted that achieving a good use of public procurement for secondary policy objectives can be quite complex, particularly in contents where capacities are limited. Hence, when leveraging public procurement to advance green and/or gender objectives should be accompanied by programmes that create the right capacities in the procurement workforce as well as guidelines that can support the coherent coexistence of both objectives (OECD, 2021[86]).

Box 2.12. Good practices: Green and gender-sensitive public procurement in the United States

Green purchasing/sustainable acquisition in the US federal government dates to 1976, with the first law establishing a preference for purchasing products made from recycled content. Today, purchasing mandates extend to, energy- and water-efficient products, bio-based products, environmentally preferable products, alternative fuel vehicles and products with reduced toxic and hazardous materials. Procurement requirements at the federal level follow sustainability mandates set up through the Federal Procurement Data System (FPDS). For purchases below USD 25 000 the Federal Acquisition Regulation mandates sustainable acquisition compliance.

There are designated environmental criteria for over 300 products. Sustainable acquisition requirements apply to products relevant to the following purchasing categories:

- electricity

- design and/or construction
- operations and maintenance
- janitorial products/services
- office supplies
- furniture
- cafeteria ware/services
- fleet management (vehicles)
- garments, uniforms, beddings and linens
- meetings and conference services
- IT equipment.

Besides green and sustainable purchasing, the United States government has also established socio-economic goals for procurements; which include purchasing from small businesses; from businesses that employ people with disabilities; as well as indigenous- or women-led businesses.

Source: (OECD, 2015[87]).

2.5.3. Women's role in sustainable consumption

Research shows that women tend to be more sustainable consumers and are more sensitive to ecological, environmental and health concerns (Johnsson-Latham, 2007[88]); (Kaenzig, Heinzle and Wüstenhagen, 2013[89]); (Khan and Trivedi, 2015[90]); (Bulut, Kökalan Çımrin and Doğan, 2017[91]). Women are more likely to recycle, minimise waste, buy organic food and eco-labelled products and engage in water and energy savings initiatives at the household level (Yaccato and Jaeger, 2003[92]). A 2008 OECD Household survey indicated that men were more likely to separate metal wastes, but not other material, even though differences in waste separation practices by sex do exist between countries as well as in relation to geographical locations (Palatnik et al., 2014[93]). Moreover, there appear to be differentiated response to financial incentives for waste reduction between men and women, with women being less responsive (Ashenmiller, 2011[94]).

The above findings are repeated in other studies. Women in Denmark seem to be more responsive to more sustainable waste management solutions. Depending on location and income, women are less sceptic than men on frequently using the recycling centre, and are more likely to accept sorting recyclables and bio-waste as part of their household waste disposal ritual compared to men. Men, on the other hand, seem not to be very engaged in recycling and pay less consideration to the environmental impact of their lifestyle choices (Nainggolan et al., 2019[95]).

When asked about preferences for goods and services, for instance when selecting electronic products, women in Denmark seem to prefer those that have an end-of-life feature (that is, the ability of the product to be reused, remanufactured or recycled). Additionally, women would be more open to paying a premium price if the product purchased was more environmentally friendly. Men would also be willing to pay a supplementary amount, but only if that was very low (Atlason, Giacalone and Parajuly, 2017[96]).

Acknowledging the gender differentiated behavioural preferences in household consumption, and waste generation and prevention, should be taken into consideration when designing effective public communications campaigns and promoting eco-labelling. Greece's awareness raising actions under the CEAP should integrate a gender-sensitive approach, adapting the messaging to different social groups, as well as engaging with business, media and civil society to promote positive and more sustainable consumption patterns.

In addition, providing incentives, as scheduled, to reduce urban waste by awarding citizens to reuse and recycle is a positive step. Linking these incentives to discounts on municipal services such as access to day-care, access to public transport etc., if designed in a gender-sensitive manner, could both support and promote women's sustainable behaviour.

2.5.4. Equal representation in circular economy leadership

Evidence suggests that women's participation in decision making can lead to better environmental outcomes in the public and private sectors (Strumskyte, Ramos Magaña and Bendig, 2022[75]). Supporting women's engagement in circular economy could assist in acknowledging women's contribution to waste and resource recovery, while also guaranteeing gender considerations to be taken into account when designing future policies and actions.

The Greek GEAP includes a multi-level governance mechanism, with the establishment of a circular economy co-ordination body, a National Observatory for Circular Economy, and a "Circular Coalition for Greece". These bodies, which guarantee stakeholder participation from public authorities, regional and local governments, private sector and academia, complement and support the inter-ministerial Committee on Circular Economy. Guaranteeing a gender equal participation in these bodies could allow for better representation of women's perspectives when discussing and designing financial and other incentives for companies, developing indicators to monitor progress, as well as promoting awareness and information campaigns.

In addition, these bodies could explore other initiatives that could strengthen women's participation in a circular economy. For example, the Government of South Australia has developed a "Women in Circular Economy Leadership Award" in an attempt to recognise women's positive contribution to local waste and resource recovery industry. Women are invited to submit their innovative ideas in one of the following categories:

- Reforming household waste through innovative practices
- Reducing and avoiding food waste and developing industries
- Reforming packaging and single-use items
- Developing the circular economy in business
- Preparing for disaster waste management.

The project must indicate the relevance and benefits to local business, and is directed to women already engaged in circular economy activities. The award guarantees financial assistance of up to AUS 5,000 and mentoring by experiences women executive leaders (Green Industries SA, n.d.[97]).

2.6. Women as agents for biodiversity conservation

Greece is rich in biodiversity, hosting a large variety of plants and species, many of which are endemic (IUCN, n.d.[98]). Yet biodiversity loss is an established phenomenon in the country, with the main causes being urbanisation, habitat fragmentation, pollution, invasive alien species, climate change and fires. Despite the country's framework being in line with international commitments, Greece needs to improve the national monitoring system, as well as mainstream biodiversity considerations in economic sectors, including especially agriculture and fisheries, transport and tourism (OECD, 2020[7]).

Agriculture and fisheries, and tourism are two of the sectors with relatively high female labour participation in Greece, despite being male-dominated sectors. Considering women's and men's differentiated impact from biodiversity loss, and their potential role in ecosystem conservation (OECD, 2021[1]), it is imperative to incorporate gender considerations in the country's biodiversity policies.

Greece's National Biodiversity Strategy and Action Plan (2014-2019) links national targets to the Aichi Biodiversity Targets. Even though reference is made to Aichi Target 14, and women's needs, there are no explicit national targets set to integrate a gender-sensitive lens in achieving the targets (Box 2.13). It should be acknowledged, however, that the role of civil society and public consultations is enhanced, which would allow for women's presence and perspective being presented in this process (MoEE, 2014[99]). Setting gender targets when updating the national Biodiversity Action Plan, as well as collecting gender-disaggregated data, could help integrate gender equality and women's empowerment considerations in the national policy framework, in line also with the expected post-2020 global biodiversity framework.

Box 2.13. Aichi Biodiversity Target 14

Under the Biological Diversity Convention's Strategic Plan for Biodiversity 2011-2020 and the Aichi Targets, the Strategic Goal D, "Enhance the benefit to all from biodiversity and ecosystem services", Target 14, includes a reference to women:

By 2020, ecosystems that provide essential services, including services related to water, and contribute to health, livelihoods and well-being, are restored and safeguarded, taking into account the needs of women, indigenous and local communities, and the poor and vulnerable.

Source: (CBD, n.d.[100]).

Greece's Environmental Law adopted in 2020 introduced changes to the national model for the management of the country's protected areas. Following an integrated model inspired by the management structure in Austria and Finland, a new co-ordinating body was established. The "Natural Environment and Climate Change Agency" is an independent body overseen by the Ministry of Environment and Energy, with the main tasks to manage protected areas, promote sustainable development and fight climate change (OG, 2020[101]); (Tzatzaki, 2020[102]).

Even though no explicit references are included in applying a gender-sensitive approach when designing actions in relation to biodiversity and safeguarding protected areas, the Agency is finalising a Gender Action Plan, with which it will monitor the gender-balance in management and administrative positions. Already, the Agency's management positions are distributed in a gender-balanced way, with four out of nine Management Board members being female. The two Directorates overseeing the regional Management Authorities of Protected Areas are also led by one male and one female Director; and two of the five Heads of the Management Authorities appointed are also female (NECCA, n.d.[103]).

References

Agroinformacion (2022), "La Rioja fomenta la igualdad de género, el relevo generacional y la sostenibilidad en su Ley de Agricultura y Ganadería", *agroinformacion.com*, https://agroinformacion.com/la-rioja-fomenta-la-igualdad-de-genero-relevo-generacional-y-sostenibilidad-en-su-ley-de-agricultura-y-ganaderia/ (accessed on 18 January 2022). [54]

Aragón, F., J. Rud and G. Toews (2018), "Resource shocks, employment, and gender: Evidence from the collapse of the UK coal industry", *Labour Economics*, Vol. 52, pp. 54-67, https://doi.org/10.1016/j.labeco.2018.03.007. [25]

Ashenmiller, B. (2011), "The Effect of Bottle Laws on Income: New Empirical Results", *The American Economic Review*, Vol. 101/3, pp. 60-64, http://www.jstor.org/stable/29783715. [94]

Atlason, R., D. Giacalone and K. Parajuly (2017), "Product design in the circular economy: Users' perception of end-of-life scenarios for electrical and electronic appliances", *Journal of Cleaner Production*, Vol. 168, pp. 1059-1069, https://doi.org/10.1016/j.jclepro.2017.09.082. [96]

Ayuntamiento de Madrd (2019), *Propuesta de fincionamiento del foro Madrd solicaria durante el ejercicio 2019*, https://www.madrid.es/UnidadesDescentralizadas/FondosEuropeos/madrid_es/EspecialInformativo/Cooperacion%20internacional%20desarrollo/Fichero/propuesta_funcionamiento_FMS_2019.pdf (accessed on 17 January 2022). [24]

Botta, E. (2019), "A review of "Transition Management" strategies: Lessons for advancing the green low-carbon transition", *OECD Green Growth Papers*, No. 2019/04, OECD Publishing, Paris, https://doi.org/10.1787/4617a02b-en. [74]

Bové, H. et al. (2019), "Ambient black carbon particles reach the fetal side of human placenta", *Nature Communications*, Vol. 10/1, https://doi.org/10.1038/s41467-019-11654-3. [11]

Bulut, Z., F. Kökalan Çımrin and O. Doğan (2017), "Gender, generation and sustainable consumption: Exploring the behaviour of consumers from Izmir, Turkey", *International Journal of Consumer Studies*, Vol. 41/6, pp. 597-604, https://doi.org/10.1111/ijcs.12371. [91]

C3E International and IEA (2019), *Status Report on Gender Equality in the Energy Sector*, https://www.cleanenergyministerial.org/sites/default/files/2019-06/Status%20Report%20on%20Gender%20Equality%20in%20the%20Energy%20Sector_0.pdf. [64]

Carlsson Kanyama, A., J. Nässén and R. Benders (2021), "Shifting expenditure on food, holidays, and furnishings could lower greenhouse gas emissions by almost 40%", *Journal of Industrial Ecology*, Vol. 25/6, pp. 1602-1616, https://doi.org/10.1111/jiec.13176. [17]

CBD (n.d.), *Aichi Biodiversity Targets*, https://www.cbd.int/sp/targets/ (accessed on 2 February 2022). [100]

Chateau, J., R. Bibas and E. Lanzi (2018), "Impacts of Green Growth Policies on Labour Markets and Wage Income Distribution: A General Equilibrium Application to Climate and Energy Policies", *OECD Environment Working Papers*, No. 137, OECD Publishing, Paris, https://doi.org/10.1787/ea3696f4-en. [73]

Chateau, J. and E. Mavroeidi (2020), "The jobs potential of a transition towards a resource efficient and circular economy", *OECD Environment Working Papers*, No. 167, OECD Publishing, Paris, https://doi.org/10.1787/28e768df-en. [71]

Chiappini, S. and M. De Rosa (2011), "Consuming rural development policies: Are there gender differences in Italian agriculture?", *Agricultural Economics Review*, Vol. 12/1, https://doi.org/10.22004/ag.econ.178214. [49]

Czap, N. et al. (2018), "Conforming to or defying gender stereotypes? Empathy nudging vs. financial incentives in environmental context", *Papers in Natural Resources*, Vol. 981, https://digitalcommons.unl.edu/natrespapers/981. [22]

Diehl, K. and P. Cerny (2021), *Women on the Move: Sustainable Mobility and Gender*,
https://eu.boell.org/en/women-on-the-move-sustainable-mobility-and-gender (accessed on
1 February 2022).
[32]

Dinis, I. et al. (2015), "Organic agriculture values and practices in Portugal and Italy", *Agricultural
Systems*, Vol. 136, pp. 39-45, https://doi.org/10.1016/j.agsy.2015.01.007.
[48]

DISER (n.d.), "Advancing Women in STEM strategy", *Australian Government, Department of
Industry, Science, Energy and Resources*, https://www.industry.gov.au/data-and-
publications/advancing-women-in-stem-strategy (accessed on 13 January 2022).
[60]

Djoudi, H. et al. (2016), "Beyond dichotomies: Gender and intersecting inequalities in climate
change studies", *Ambio*, Vol. 45/S3, pp. 248-262, https://doi.org/10.1007/s13280-016-0825-2.
[3]

DoAFM (2021), *Minister McConalogue announces supports to promote gender equality in
farming*, https://www.gov.ie/en/press-release/c9232-minister-mcconalogue-announces-
supports-to-promote-gender-equality-in-farming/ (accessed on 12 January 2022).
[52]

EC (2021), *Commission Staff Working Document on the territorial just transition plans*,
https://ec.europa.eu/regional_policy/sources/thefunds/jtf/swd_territ_just_trans_plan_en.pdf.
[26]

EC (2021), *GPP National Action Plans*,
https://ec.europa.eu/environment/gpp/action_plan_en.htm (accessed on 16 January 2022).
[83]

EC (2016), *Buying green! A handbook on green public procurement*,
https://doi.org/10.2779/246106.
[81]

EC (n.d.), *European Climate Law*, https://ec.europa.eu/clima/eu-action/european-green-
deal/european-climate-law_en (accessed on 29 April 2022).
[9]

EIGE (n.d.), *Agriculture and rural development*, https://eige.europa.eu/gender-
mainstreaming/policy-areas/agriculture-and-rural-development.
[45]

EmpowerMed (n.d.), *EMPOWERING WOMEN TO TAKE ACTION AGAINST ENERGY
POVERTY*, https://www.empowermed.eu/ (accessed on 15 January 2022).
[23]

European Parliament, T. et al. (2019), *The professional status of rural women in the EU*,
https://www.europarl.europa.eu/RegData/etudes/STUD/2019/608868/IPOL_STU(2019)60886
8_EN.pdf.
[44]

Field, C. (ed.) (2014), *Climate Change 2014: Impacts, Adaptation, and Vulnerability. Summaries,
Frequently Asked Questions, and Cross-Chapter Boxes. A*, World Meteorological
Organization, https://www.ipcc.ch/site/assets/uploads/2018/03/WGIIAR5-
IntegrationBrochure_FINAL-1.pdf.
[4]

FIT (n.d.), *Finacial Literacy and New Business Models to Boost Women Entrepreneurship
Possibilities*, https://the-fitproject.eu/.
[79]

Gkasouka, M. and X. Foulidi (2018), *The Greek farmer woman: Capturing participation,
problems, challenges and policy proposals to encourage women's participation in the
agricultural sector and greek rural areas*, National Printing House, https://isotita.gr/wp-
content/uploads/2018/02/%CE%97-
%CE%95%CE%BB%CE%BB%CE%B7%CE%BD%CE%AF%CE%B4%CE%B1-
%CE%B1%CE%B3%CF%81%CF%8C%CF%84%CE%B9%CF%83%CF%83%CE%B1.pdf.
[43]

Green Industries SA (n.d.), *Women in Circular Economy Leadership Award*, [97]
https://www.greenindustries.sa.gov.au/women-in-ce-leadership-award (accessed on
11 January 2022).

Grünewald, P. and M. Diakonova (2020), "Societal differences, activities, and performance: [16]
Examining the role of gender in electricity demand in the United Kingdom", *Energy Research
& Social Science*, Vol. 69, https://doi.org/10.1016/j.erss.2020.101719.

Hossain, M. et al. (2017), "Women in the boardroom and their impact on climate change related [61]
disclosure", *Social Responsibility Journal*, Vol. 13/4, pp. 828-855, https://doi.org/10.1108/srj-
11-2016-0208.

Huddart Kennedy, E., H. Krahn and N. Krogman (2015), "Are we counting what counts? A closer [15]
look at environmental concern, pro-environmental behaviour, and carbon footprint", *Local
Environment*, Vol. 20/2, https://doi.org/10.1080/13549839.2013.837039.

IEA (2020), *Gender diversity in energy: what we know and what we don't know*, [63]
https://www.iea.org/commentaries/gender-diversity-in-energy-what-we-know-and-what-we-
dont-know (accessed on 23 March 2021).

ILO (2015), *Gender equality and green jobs*, International Labour Organization. [70]

IRENA (2019), *Renewable energy: A gender perspective*, IRENA, http://www.irena.org. [59]

IUCN (n.d.), *Greece*, https://www.iucn.org/regions/europe/resources/country-focus/greece [98]
(accessed on 1 February 2022).

Jerneck, A. (2018), "What about Gender in Climate Change? Twelve Feminist Lessons from [2]
Development", *Sustainability*, Vol. 10/3, p. 627, https://doi.org/10.3390/su10030627.

Johnsson-Latham, G. (2007), *A study on gender equality as a prerequisite for sustainable [88]
development*, Report to the Environment Advisory Council, Stockholm,
http://www.sou.gov.se/mvb/.

Kaenzig, J., S. Heinzle and R. Wüstenhagen (2013), "Whatever the customer wants, the [89]
customer gets? Exploring the gap between consumer preferences and default electricity
products in Germany", *Energy Policy*, Vol. 53, https://doi.org/10.1016/j.enpol.2012.10.061.

Khan, N. and P. Trivedi (2015), "Gender Differences and Sustainable Consumption Behavior", [90]
British Journal of Marketing Studies, Vol. 3/3, pp. 29-35, https://www.eajournals.org/wp-
content/uploads/Gender-Differences-and-Sustainable-Consumption-Behavior.pdf.

London Assembly (n.d.), *Women's Night Safety Charter*, https://www.london.gov.uk/what-we- [30]
do/arts-and-culture/24-hour-london/womens-night-safety-charter (accessed on
17 January 2022).

MAPA (2021), *Luis Planas presenta el Plan Estratégico de la PAC, dotado con 47.724 millones [51]
de euros hasta 2027, que se enviará mañana a la Comisión Europea*,
https://www.mapa.gob.es/es/prensa/ultimas-noticias/luis-planas-presenta-el-plan-
estrat%C3%A9gico-de-la-pac-dotado-con-47.724-millones-de-euros-hasta-2027-que-se-
enviar%C3%A1-ma%C3%B1ana-a-la-comisi%C3%B3n-europea/tcm:30-584010 (accessed
on 18 January 2022).

Mitsios, A. et al. (2019), *Eco-Innovation Observatory - Country Profile 2018-2019: Greece*, https://ec.europa.eu/environment/ecoap/sites/default/files/field/field-country-files/eio_country_profile_2018-2019_greece.pdf. [56]

MoADF (2021), *Εθνικό Μητρώο Αγροτικών Συνεταιρισμών και άλλων συλλογικών φορέων*, http://minagric.gr/index.php/el/for-farmer-2/sillogikes-agrotikes-organoseis (accessed on 20 January 2022). [50]

MoEE (2021), *Circular Economy Action Plan*, https://ypen.gov.gr/wp-content/uploads/2021/12/SXEDIO-DRASHS-KO-FINAL_.pdf. [67]

MoEE (2021), *National Climate Law - Transition to climate neutrality and climate change adaptation*, http://www.opengov.gr/minenv/?p=12285 (accessed on 10 December 2021). [105]

MoEE (2019), *National Energy and Climate Plan - Greece*, https://ec.europa.eu/energy/sites/ener/files/el_final_necp_main_en.pdf. [6]

MoEE (2014), *National Biodiverisy Strategy & Action Plan*, https://ypen.gov.gr/wp-content/uploads/legacy/Files/Perivallon/Diaxeirisi%20Fysikoy%20Perivallontos/Biopoikilotita/20200323_ethniki_strathgiki_biodiversity.pdf. [99]

Murray, A., K. Skene and K. Haynes (2017), "The Circular Economy: An Interdisciplinary Exploration of the Concept and Application in a Global Context", *Journal of Business Ethics*, Vol. 140/3, https://doi.org/10.1007/s10551-015-2693-2. [69]

Nafilyan, V. (2019), *Gender differences in commute time and pay: A study into the gender gap for pay and commuting time, using data from the Annual Survey of Hours and Earnings*, https://www.ons.gov.uk/employmentandlabourmarket/peopleinwork/earningsandworkinghours/articles/genderdifferencesincommutetimeandpay/2019-09-04. [33]

Nainggolan, D. et al. (2019), "Consumers in a Circular Economy: Economic Analysis of Household Waste Sorting Behaviour", *Ecological Economics*, Vol. 166, p. 106402, https://doi.org/10.1016/j.ecolecon.2019.106402. [95]

NECCA (n.d.), *Natural Environment and Climate Change Agency*, https://necca.gov.gr/ (accessed on 2 February 2022). [103]

Ng, W. and A. Acker (2018), "Understanding Urban Travel Behaviour by Gender for Efficient and Equitable Transport Policies", *International Transport Forum Discussion Papers*, No. 2018/01, OECD Publishing, Paris, https://doi.org/10.1787/eaf64f94-en. [34]

OAED (2021), *Ειδικό πρόγραμμα επιχορήγησης επιχειρήσεων για την απασχόληση 3400 ανέργων, πρώην εργαζομένων στις επιχειρήσεις που επλήγησαν λόγω της απολιγνιτοποίησης στις Περιφέρειες της Δυτικής Μακεδονίας και της Πελοποννήσου*, https://www.oaed.gr/storage/apaskholisi/9ees4691o2-thfo.pdf. [28]

OECD (2022), *Self-employed with employees* (indicator), https://doi.org/10.1787/b7bf59b6-en (accessed on 29 January 2022). [77]

OECD (2022), *Self-employed without employees* (indicator), https://doi.org/10.1787/5d5d0d63-en (accessed on 29 January 2022). [78]

OECD (2021), *Entrepreneurship Policies through a Gender Lens*, OECD Studies on SMEs and Entrepreneurship, OECD Publishing, Paris, https://doi.org/10.1787/71c8f9c9-en. [76]

OECD (2021), *Gender and the Environment: Building Evidence and Policies to Achieve the SDGs*, OECD Publishing, Paris, https://doi.org/10.1787/3d32ca39-en. [1]

OECD (2021), "Gender-relevance of policies in the OECD Green Recovery Database", *OECD Policy Responses to Coronavirus (COVID-19)*, OECD Publishing, Paris, https://doi.org/10.1787/e6a03378-en. [109]

OECD (2021), *OECD SME and Entrepreneurship Outlook 2021*, OECD Publishing, Paris, https://doi.org/10.1787/97a5bbfe-en. [55]

OECD (2021), *Policy Framework for gender-sensitive public governance*, https://www.oecd.org/mcm/Policy-Framework-for-Gender-Sensitive-Public-Governance.pdf. [84]

OECD (2021), "Promoting gender equality through public procurement: Challenges and good practices", *OECD Public Governance Policy Papers*, No. 09, OECD Publishing, Paris, https://doi.org/10.1787/5d8f6f76-en. [86]

OECD (2021), "The OECD Green Recovery Database: Examining the environmental implications of COVID-19 recovery policies", *OECD Policy Responses to Coronavirus (COVID-19)*, OECD Publishing, Paris, https://doi.org/10.1787/47ae0f0d-en. [107]

OECD (2021), "Women in infrastructure: Selected stocktaking of good practices for inclusion of women in infrastructure", *OECD Public Governance Policy Papers*, No. 07, OECD Publishing, Paris, https://doi.org/10.1787/9eab66a8-en. [39]

OECD (2020), *EPOC Survey on integrating gender in environmental policies*, https://one.oecd.org/document/ENV/EPOC(2020)9/en/pdf. [5]

OECD (2020), *Gender and Environmental Statistics. Exploring available Data and Developing New Evidence Contents*, OECD, https://www.oecd.org/environment/brochure-gender-and-environmental-statistics.pdf. [58]

OECD (2020), *Global Forum on Environment: Mainstreaming Gender and Empowering Women for Environmental Sustainability - Key Outcomes [ENV/EPOC(2020)7/FINAL]*. [35]

OECD (2020), *OECD Environmental Performance Reviews: Greece 2020*, OECD Environmental Performance Reviews, OECD Publishing, Paris, https://doi.org/10.1787/cec20289-en. [7]

OECD (2020), "Research and Development Statistics: Government budget appropriations or outlays for RD (Edition 2020)", *OECD Science, Technology and R&D Statistics* (database), https://doi.org/10.1787/620bbce8-en (accessed on 10 January 2022). [108]

OECD (2019), *EPOC Survey on integrating gender in environmental policies - Chile's response*. [53]

OECD (2019), *Gender, Institutions and Development Database*, https://oe.cd/ds/GIDDB2019 (accessed on 1 December 2021). [42]

OECD (2019), *Measuring the Digital Transformation: A Roadmap for the Future*, OECD Publishing, Paris, https://doi.org/10.1787/9789264311992-en. [57]

OECD (2017), *2013 OECD Recommendation of the Council on Gender Equality in Education, Employment and Entrepreneurship*, OECD Publishing, Paris, https://doi.org/10.1787/9789264279391-en. [111]

OECD (2017), *Behavioural Insights and Public Policy: Lessons from Around the World*, OECD Publishing, Paris, https://doi.org/10.1787/9789264270480-en. [21]

OECD (2017), *Getting Infrastructure Right: A framework for better governance*, OECD Publishing, Paris, https://doi.org/10.1787/9789264272453-en. [40]

OECD (2015), *Going Green: Best Practices for Sustainable Procurement*, https://www.oecd.org/gov/public-procurement/Going_Green_Best_Practices_for_Sustainable_Procurement.pdf. [87]

OECD (2015), *OECD Recommendation of the Council on Public Procurement*, OECD Publishing, https://www.oecd.org/gov/public-procurement/OECD-Recommendation-on-Public-Procurement.pdf. [85]

OECD (2011), *Greening Household Behaviour: The Role of Public Policy*, OECD Studies on Environmental Policy and Household Behaviour, OECD Publishing, Paris, https://doi.org/10.1787/9789264096875-en. [110]

OECD (n.d.), *RE-CIRCLE: resource efficiency and circular economy*, https://www.oecd.org/environment/waste/recircle.htm (accessed on 12 November 2021). [68]

OECD (n.d.), *Recommendation of the Council on the Governance of Infrastructure*, http://legalinstruments.oecd.org. [41]

OECD (forthcoming), *Women in environmental leadership*. [106]

OG (2022), *Law 4936/2022 - Εθνικός Κλιματικός Νόμος - Μετάβαση στην κλιματική ουδετερότητα και προσαρμογή στην κλιματική αλλαγή, επείγουσες διατάξεις για την αντιμετώπιση της ενεργειακής κρίσης και την προστασία του περιβάλλοντος*, Official Government Gazette. [8]

OG (2021), *Ministerial Decision ΥΠΕΝ/ΓΔΕ/89335/5599 "Approval of the National Action Plan against Energy Poverty, according to para.1 of art.25 of Law 4342/2015" (OJ B 4447/28.09.2021)*, Offical Government Gazette. [19]

OG (2021), *Έγκριση Σχεδίου Δράσης για τις Πράσινες Δημόσιες Συμβάσεις (JMD 14900/2021)*, Official Government Gazette, http://www.mindev.gov.gr/wp-content/uploads/2021/03/%CE%A6%CE%95%CE%9A466%CE%92_08022021_%CE%91%CE%A0%CE%9F%CE%A6%CE%91%CE%A3%CE%97_%CE%95%CE%93%CE%9A%CE%A1%CE%99%CE%A3%CE%97-%CE%A3%CE%A7%CE%95%CE%94%CE%99%CE%9F%CE%A5-%CE%94%CE%A1%CE%91%CE%A3%CE%97%CE%A3_. [82]

OG (2020), *Law 4685/2020 - Εκσυγχρονισμός περιβαλλοντικής νομοθεσίας, ενσωμάτωση στην ελληνική νομοθεσία των Οδηγιών 2018/844 και 2019/692 του Ευρωπαϊκού Κοινοβουλίου και του Συμβουλίου και λοιπές διατάξεις*, Official Government Gazette. [101]

OG (2018), *Joint Ministerial Decision 1915/2018 "Amendment of No. 48963/2012 (B 2703) JMD, No. 167563/2013 (B 964) JMD and No. 170225/2014 (B135) MD, which have been issued by authorisation of Law 4014/2011, in compliance with Directive 2014/52*, Official Government Gazette. [38]

OG (2014), *Ministerial Decision 170225/2014 "Specialisation of the contents of the environment licencing folders for works and activities under Category A of the 1958/2012 Decision of the Minister of Environment, Energy and Climate Change (B 21)...*, Official Government Gazette. [37]

Ostry, J. et al. (2018), *Economic Gains from Gender Inclusion: New Mechanisms, New Evidence; IMF Staff Discussion Notes No. 18/06; October 9, 2018; by J. D. Ostry, J. Alvarez, R. Espinoza, and C. Papageorgiou.* [72]

Otro Tiempo Otro Planeta (n.d.), *Cuida el medioambiente, recicla tu aceite*, https://otrotiempo-otroplaneta.org/ (accessed on 15 December 2021). [80]

Palatnik, R. et al. (2014), "Greening Household Behaviour and Waste", *OECD Environment Working Papers*, No. 76, OECD Publishing, Paris, https://doi.org/10.1787/5jxrclmxnfr8-en. [93]

Petrova, S. (2017), "Illuminating austerity: Lighting poverty as an agent and signifier of the Greek crisis", *European Urban and Regional Studies*, Vol. 25/4, pp. 360-372, https://doi.org/10.1177/0969776417720250. [12]

Petrova, S. and N. Simcock (2019), "Gender and energy: domestic inequities reconsidered", *Social & Cultural Geography*, Vol. 22/6, pp. 849-867, https://doi.org/10.1080/14649365.2019.1645200. [13]

Post, C., N. Rahman and E. Rubow (2011), "Green Governance: Boards of Directors' Composition and Environmental Corporate Social Responsibility", *Business & Society*, Vol. 50/1, pp. 189-223, https://doi.org/10.1177/0007650310394642. [62]

Räty, R. and A. Carlsson-Kanyama (2010), "Energy consumption by gender in some European countries", *Energy Policy*, Vol. 38/1, pp. 646-649, https://doi.org/10.1016/j.enpol.2009.08.010. [112]

Robinson, C. (2019), "Energy poverty and gender in England: A spatial perspective", *Geoforum*, Vol. 104, pp. 222-233, https://doi.org/10.1016/j.geoforum.2019.05.001. [10]

SAAMO West-Vlaanderen (n.d.), *samen uitsluiting aanpakken in West-Vlaanderen*, https://www.saamo.be/west-vlaanderen/ (accessed on 17 January 2022). [18]

Sachs, C. (2006), "Rural women and the environment.", in *Rural gender relations: issues and case studies*, CABI, Wallingford, https://doi.org/10.1079/9780851990309.0288. [47]

Samek Lodovici, M. et al. (2012), *The role of women in the green economy-The issue of mobility*, European Union, http://www.europarl.europa.eu/studies. [31]

SDAM (n.d.), *Το Σχέδιο Δράσης του ΥΠΕΝ για την καταπολέμηση της ενεργειακής φτώχειας πορβλέπει επιπλέον 10% ενίσχυση για τις λιγνιτικές περιοχές*, https://www.sdam.gr/index.php/node/325 (accessed on 10 January 2022). [20]

STEMReturners (n.d.), *STEM Returners*, https://www.stemreturners.com/the-programme/ (accessed on 17 January 2022). [66]

Stevenson, G. et al. (2021), *Women and the Net Zero economy: A briefing on changes in garment, agriculture and energy supply chains*, https://assets.publishing.service.gov.uk/government/uploads/system/uploads/attachment_data/file/980198/Guidance3-Women--Net-Zero-Economy-Briefing1.pdf (accessed on 15 January 2022). [27]

Strumskyte, S., S. Ramos Magaña and H. Bendig (2022), "Women's leadership in environmental action", *OECD Environment Working Papers*, No. 193, OECD Publishing, Paris, https://doi.org/10.1787/f0038d22-en. [75]

Tjørring, L. (2016), "We forgot half of the population! The significance of gender in Danish energy renovation projects", *Energy Research & Social Science*, Vol. 22, pp. 115-124, https://doi.org/10.1016/j.erss.2016.08.008.   [104]

Tzanne, M. (2022), *Οι big μπιζνες 60 γυναικών στην ηλιακή ενέργεια*.   [29]

Tzatzaki, V. (2020), "Recent Developments in Environmental Law in Greece: A Commentary", *International Journal of Environmental Protection and Policy*, Vol. 8/3, p. 66, https://doi.org/10.11648/j.ijepp.20200803.13.   [102]

U.S. Department of Energy et al. (n.d.), *The U.S. Clean Energy Education & Empowerment (C3E) Initiative*, https://c3e.org/ (accessed on 17 January 2022).   [65]

Umaerus, P., M. Högvall Nordin and G. Lidestav (2019), "Do female forest owners think and act "greener"?", *Forest Policy and Economics*, Vol. 99, pp. 52-58, https://doi.org/10.1016/j.forpol.2017.12.001.   [46]

Urban Development Vienna (2013), *Gender Mainstreaming in Urban Planning and Urban Development*, https://www.wien.gv.at/stadtentwicklung/studien/pdf/b008358.pdf (accessed on 4 November 2020).   [36]

Urban, J. and M. Ščasný (2012), "Exploring domestic energy-saving: The role of environmental concern and background variables", *Energy Policy*, Vol. 47, pp. 69-80, https://doi.org/10.1016/j.enpol.2012.04.018.   [14]

Yaccato, J. and J. Jaeger (2003), *The 80% Minority: Reaching the Real World of Women Consumers*, Viking Canada.   [92]

Notes

[1] The analysis in this report covers not only environmental sectors (i.e. producers of environmental products, such as goods and services produced for environmental protection or natural resource management), but also environment-related sectors and activities (i.e. other economic sectors that have an environmental impact, e.g. agriculture).

[2] Carbon budgets represent the total amount of emissions that may be emitted in a country during a five-year period, measured in tonnes of carbon dioxide equivalent.

[3] Social infrastructure refers to infrastructure that supports the development of the human resource potential and ameliorates living conditions. It includes, but is not limited to, infrastructure relating to education; health; and water supply, sanitation and sewerage.

3 Assessing gender equality policies and their role in advancing environmental sustainability in Greece

This chapter assesses gender equality legislation and policies and practices for environmental sustainability in Greece, with a focus on women's economic empowerment in the green economy. It identifies gaps under the gender-environment nexus, proposes ways of mainstreaming gender in national policies, and includes good practices in other OECD countries for tackling discrimination, increasing women's participation in green jobs, and investing in girls' and women's education and training in green skills and eco-innovation.

3.1. Gender equality in Greece

Greek Law 4531/2018, which ratifies the Council of Europe Convention on preventing and combating violence against women (Istanbul Convention), and Law 4606/2019, on promoting substantive gender equality, constitute a sound legislative framework for advancing gender equality. Additional legislative measures introduced in 2021 provide a supporting framework for work-life balance. Policy initiatives to support women's economic empowerment and labour market entry are also in the pipeline. As a result of these legal initiatives, Greece now ranks among 12 OECD countries at the top of the World Bank's 2022 Women, Business and the Law Index, which collects data on laws and regulations that affect women's economic opportunity (Figure 3.1).

Figure 3.1. Twelve OECD countries top the World Bank WBL Index for 2022

2022 World Bank Women, Business and Law Index

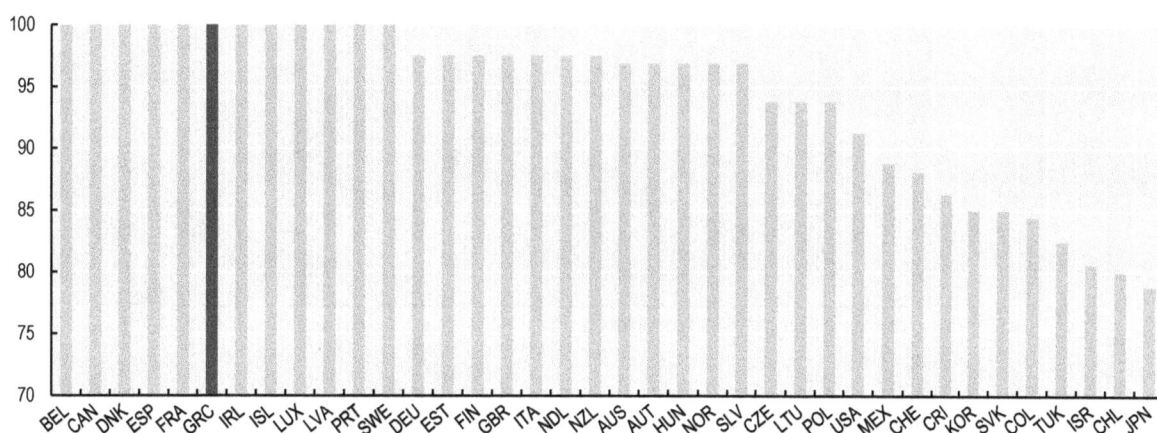

Note: Highest ranking is 100. Countries ranked for eight indicators: mobility, workplace, pay, marriage, parenthood, entrepreneurship, assets and pension. Total WBL Index equals the average of the eight indicators.
Source: (World Bank, 2022[1]) (World Bank, 2022[2]).

Inequalities persist at the implementation level, however. This is apparent when looking at the OECD Gender Data Portal, which collects data on cross-country indicators in education, employment, entrepreneurship and governance, among others (Box 3.1). In 2021, Greece ranked last among EU member states on gender equality, with this score remaining relatively stable over the last decade (EIGE, 2021[3]). The OECD Social Institutions and Gender Index (SIGI), which measures discrimination against women in social institutions across 180 countries, confirms Greece's low scores when compared with other OECD members over four dimensions: discrimination in the family, restricted physical integrity, restricted access to productive and financial resource, and restricted civil liberties (Figure 3.2) (OECD, 2019[4]).

Box 3.1. The OECD Gender Initiative

The OECD Gender Initiative (2010) examines existing barriers to gender equality in specific policy areas, monitors countries' progress in promoting gender equality, and provides good practices to that effect. The initiative is supported by the OECD Gender Data Portal, which includes a series of indicators for education (11 indicators), employment (16 indicators), entrepreneurship (11 indicators), governance

---

(10 indicators), health (10 indicators) and development (7 indicators), allowing OECD members and other countries to identify where policy actions to achieve gender equality are needed.

Source: (OECD, n.d.[5]).

Figure 3.2. Gender discrimination in Greece remains high compared to best practice

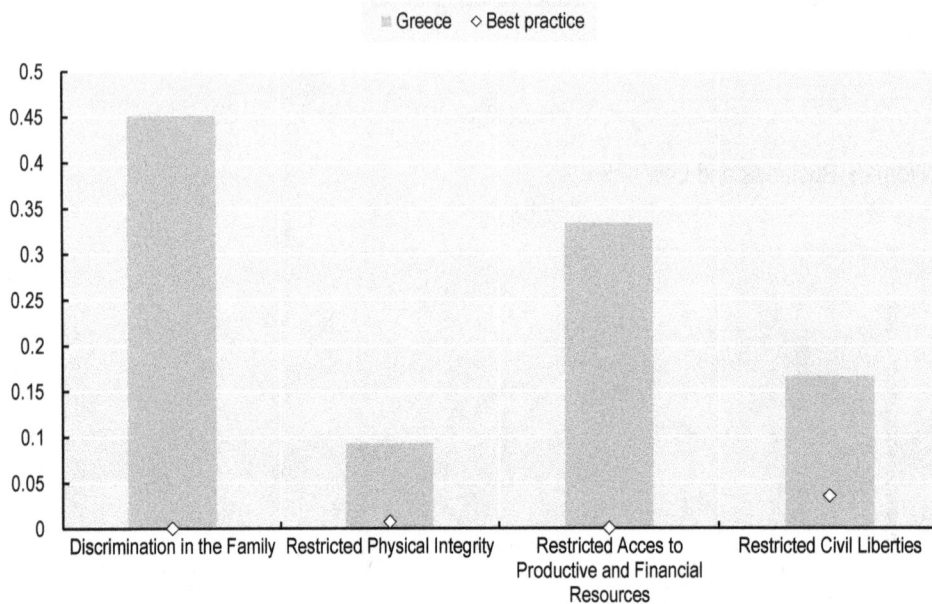

Source: OECD Social Institutions and Gender Index (OECD, 2019[6]).

Greece's recently updated Gender Equality Action Plan (GEAP), the National Action Plan for Gender Equality 2021-2025, is co-ordinated by the General Secretariat for Demography, Family Policy and Gender Equality in the Ministry of Labour and Social Affairs, which oversees its implementation. The GEAP is prepared in consultation with line ministries and the National Council for Gender Equality, a collective advisory body with representatives from national, regional and local government bodies, gender experts and civil society. It supports the realisation of the national legislative framework on gender equality in the following priority areas:

- Combatting gender-based violence through implementation of the Istanbul Convention, eliminating violence in the workplace, and enforcing and upgrading support structures for victims;

- Increasing women's participation in public policy making, women's representation in senior management in the public and private sectors, and educating women and girls to support them in reaching leadership positions;

- Supporting women's economic empowerment by increasing women's labour participation, reconciling professional and family life, advancing women's entrepreneurship, and supporting education and training for women and girls in research and development (R&D);

- Mainstreaming gender in sectoral policies by incorporating an intersectional approach, minimising the risk of social exclusion for women, promoting gender equality in health, sports and culture (media), and enhancing statistical data collection and surveys to support analysis from a gender perspective.

Greece's GEAP proposes indicators to measure the implementation of the Istanbul Convention, the International Labour Organization Convention on Violence and Harassment in the World of Work, and other policies combatting gender-based violence; women's participation in national and European decision-making bodies; women's leadership in the public and private sectors; women's labour participation by economic activity; work-life balance; gender pay gaps; gender-sensitive budgeting initiatives; and sectoral and academic gender equality action plans (MoL, 2021[7]).

The Greek Ministry of Environment and Energy (MoEE) contributes to the GEAP's design and implementation. However, other than acknowledging the negative impact of environmental degradation on women's empowerment and gender equality, and the role women play in advancing environmental sustainability, no concrete commitments or actions are set out by the MoEE. The MoEE follows national laws with regard to representation in public consultations, state-owned enterprises' management boards, and energy communities (see section 2.2.2), and applies the EU's non-discrimination principle (i.e. allowing all individuals an equal and fair chance to access opportunities available in society) in its policies and programmes, but much more could be done to include gender considerations in the design of environmental and climate policies, as described in Chapter 2. A consistently stated commitment to gender-sensitive and gender-responsible policies could help raise awareness within the public administration and promote the integration of a gender lens in all policies.

Beyond the MoEE's compliance with the GEAP, other measures and initiatives could benefit from an environmental sustainability lens, which would enhance Greece's achievement of sustainable development and transition to a low-carbon economy. As seen in Table 3.1, several policy actions included in the GEAP could directly and indirectly support women's inclusion in economic activities overall, and in environment-related and green activities more specifically.

Table 3.1. Greece's Gender Equality Action Plan 2021-2025

Measures with possible environmental considerations

Priority Area	Actions in place (responsible ministry)	Forthcoming actions/ proposals (responsible ministry)	Possible environmental considerations
Combating gender-based violence			
	Application of the ILO Convention 190 on violence and harassment at work (Ministry of Labour and Social Affairs)		
Increasing women's participation in public life			
Leadership and Decision making	25% quota for management board members to limited corporations, and diversity principles (non-discrimination) (Ministry of Finance)		Systematically pursue women's participation in leadership and decision-making positions in environment-related bodies (e.g. National Circular Economy Observatory; National Observatory for Climate Change Adaptation, etc.)
	Economic and Social Committee - 1/3 quota at Plenary and Executive Committee (Ministry of Finance)		
	National Council for Research, Technology and Innovation gender balance (8 male and 7		

Priority Area	Actions in place (responsible ministry)	Forthcoming actions/ proposals (responsible ministry)	Possible environmental considerations
	female members) (Ministry of Development and Investment)		
Supporting women's economic empowerment			
Employment / Labour policies	Labour force specialisation, reskilling and upskilling through a revised skills model (Ministry of Labour and Social Affairs)	Active labour market policies targeting vulnerable groups (Ministry of Labour and Social Affairs)	• Develop a national green skills strategy, for advancing green skills for all. • Advance training on green skills for green occupations. Include more focused and targeted programming for women. • Encourage reskilling and upskilling both for female workers already in the job market (to pursue better green jobs) and for unemployed female workers and/or those re-entering the market.
	Labour law: promoting work flexibility, allowing for working overtime one day and less on another, only after agreement between employer and employee (Ministry of Labour and Social Affairs)		
	14-day paternity leave for fathers wishing to apply, combined with a six-month prohibition of dismissal (Ministry of Labour and Social Affairs)		
	Specialised actions to increase women's labour participation and entrepreneurship in cultural heritage and creative economy. Also develop skills for women's handcrafting (Ministry of Culture and Sports)		Support maintaining women's traditional knowledge which is often linked to the creative economy in agriculture
Women's entrepreneurship		«Financial support to island entrepreneurship», to add target: «Promote female entrepreneurship in small and remote islands with special emphasis in supporting local economy and traditional products» (Ministry of Maritime Affairs and Insular Policy)	
	More favourable terms for women-led farming co-operatives (Ministry of Rural Development and Food)	Co-ordinate actions between Ministry of Rural Development and Food and General Secretariat for Gender Equality, on actions to support women farmers, and women in green jobs (Ministry of Rural	Promote financial incentives (i.e. grants) to support women's participation in farming; increase women's knowledge and adoption of innovative farming techniques (see section 2.3.3)

Priority Area	Actions in place (responsible ministry)	Forthcoming actions/ proposals (responsible ministry)	Possible environmental considerations
		Development and Food and Ministry of Labour and Social Affairs)	
Gender pay gap / equal pay principle	Non-discrimination principle of equal pay for equal work or work of equal value (Ministry of Labour and Social Affairs)		
Education	Skills labs in primary and secondary education - life skills, soft skills, technology skills, with a focus in four areas: well-being, environment, social responsibility and creativity. Structure based on SDGs, Well-being focus on gender equality (Ministry of Education and Religious Affairs)	Develop actions for schoolgirls and STEM, by breaking stereotypes in knowledge, achievement and carrier choices. Support through mentoring, role models, linking with female university students (Ministry of Education and Religious Affairs)	Further explore the extent of boys and girls interest in 'green jobs', the development of related skills (such as STEM skills, personal adaptability and creative problem-solving) and the influence of their awareness of environmental challenges in future thinking
Women in innovation	Greek Innovation lab for Women (Ministry of Development and Investment, Ministry of Labour and Social Affairs)	Encourage women to participate more in Artificial Intelligence (AI) (Ministry of Education and Religious Affairs)	• Target women's further engagement in environmental innovation; provide funding opportunities for women's entrepreneurship in eco-innovation • Introduce a "green" stream at the future programming of the Greek Innovation Lab for Women
	Elevate Greece awards for Female Innovative Entrepreneurship (Ministry of Development and Investment)	Encourage women and girls to follow vocational education and training in specialisations linked to technology, ICT and other professions with low female participation (Ministry of Education and Religious Affairs]	• Collect statistical data by sex on start-ups and innovative entrepreneurship • Increase women's concentration in scientific/technical positions in eco-innovation and green entrepreneurship, through targeted programming, training and skills development • Increase women's presence in Research Centres overseen by the Gen. Secretariat for Research & Innovation (Ministry of Development and Investment)
Mainstreaming gender in sectoral policies			
Gender budgeting		Develop gender budgeting (Ministry of Finance, Ministry of Labour and Social Affairs)	Consider integrating both green and gender budgeting
Mainstreaming gender	Gender Equality Digital Map - platform and depository with information and actions of all Gender Equality Committees at national, regional, local level, in academia and in gender equality agencies (all ministries)		

Priority Area	Actions in place (responsible ministry)	Forthcoming actions/ proposals (responsible ministry)	Possible environmental considerations
Mainstreaming gender through public consultations	Economic and Social Committee to hold open dialogue with civil society, including women's organisations or organisations on gender equality, in advance of consultations for national legislation (Ministry of Finance)		Raise awareness and encourage women-led organisations to participate in environmental public consultations
Mainstreaming gender in education		Complete establishment of Gender Equality Committees at Universities, as well as of a complaint desk for issues linked to gender equality (Ministry of Education and Religious Affairs)	
		Information and awareness raising on gender equality in vocational education and training (Ministry of Education and Religious Affairs)	
		Specialised focus for increasing women's participation to second-chance schools and other initiatives or re-entering the educational system (and therefore minimising their social exclusion) (Ministry of Education and Religious Affairs)	
Statistics	labour participation, gender pay gap, demographic data, parameters such as age, geography (Statistics Authority and line ministries)		Develop gender-environment indicators to follow women's participation in environmental and environment-related sectors and green economy; measure women's leadership and decision-making in environment-related positions etc.

Note: The information in this table is not exhaustive of all actions in the Greek Gender Equality Action Plan. Only actions that could improve women's economic empowerment in green growth, and could be further developed via a gender lens, are included.
Source: Authors compilation based on (MoL, 2021[7]).

3.2. Applying an environment lens to the Greek Gender Equality Action Plan

3.2.1. Supporting women's economic empowerment

Women's labour force participation in Greece remains low compared to the OECD average. Moreover, Greece is one of the European OECD members with the widest gender gap in labour force participation, with men at 75.5% and women at 59.3% (Figure 3.3).

Figure 3.3. Labour force participation in OECD countries, by gender

2020 data

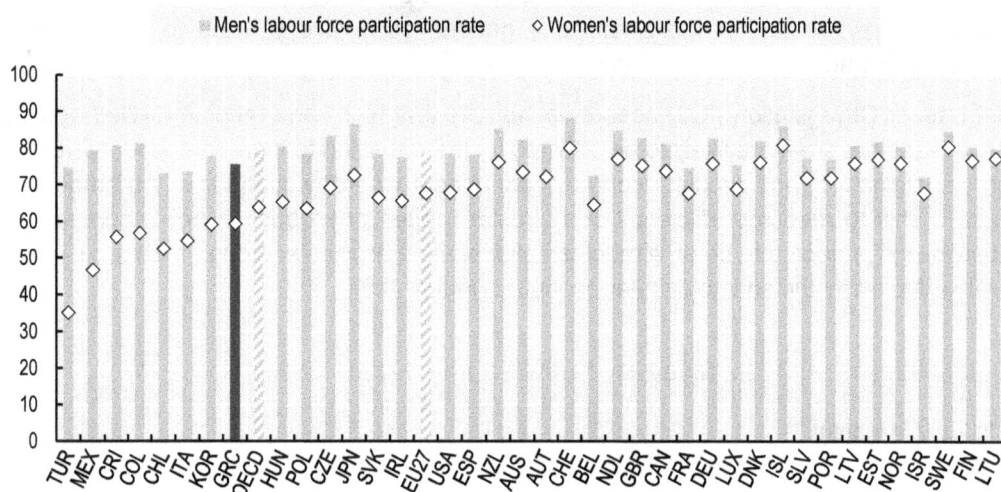

Source: (OECD, 2022[8]).

In Greece and across OECD countries, health and education are the only female-dominated employment sectors. Women are relatively present in wholesale and retail trade, agriculture, and in accommodation and food service activities. Women's presence is minimal in sectors such as mining and quarrying, utilities, construction, financial and insurance, and transport and logistics – sectors that mark high in GHG emissions, pollution and other forms of environmental damage (Figure 3.4).

Figure 3.4. Percentage of female employment in economic activities in Greece and other OECD countries

August 2021 data

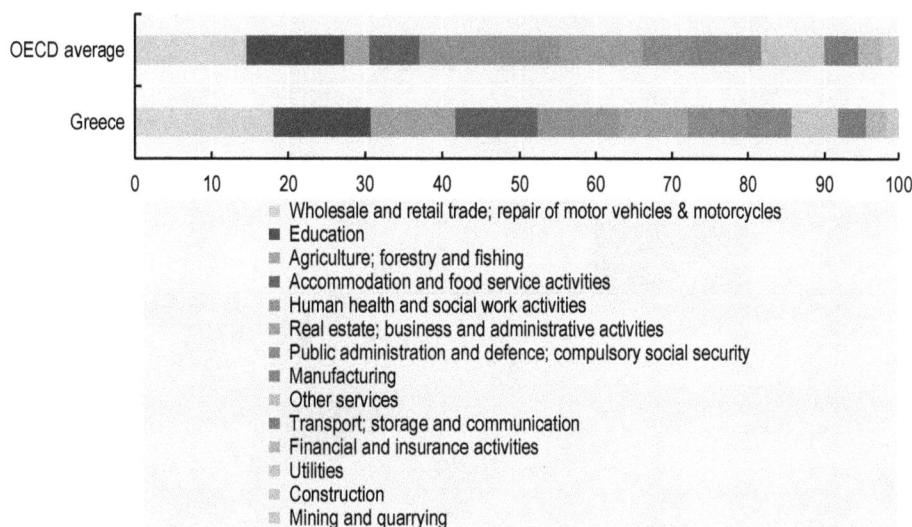

Note: Female employment by economic activity as a percentage of total female employment.
Source: ILOSTAT.

Estimates predict that the majority of green jobs created in the EU will be in construction, manufacturing and engineering (Gil, Sánchez López and Murillo, 2013[9]). The green transition and technological advances are expected to affect business opportunities in these sectors as well as the nature of related jobs and skills profiles. As women's presence in these sectors is already limited (in both OECD and EU countries) women may be further marginalised if gender-responsive policies to guarantee women's inclusion in the green transition are not adopted.

International Labour Organization (ILO) scenarios indicate that high- and medium-skilled occupations in male-dominated sectors are more likely to be affected by the transition to a green economy (ILO, 2019[10]). Under energy sustainability and circular economy scenarios – whereby changes in the amount of energy produced and a shift to resource efficiency and circular modes of production are assumed – women's uptake of new jobs is projected to be on a much smaller scale than men's, though men are expected to be more severely affected by the shift to circular economy (Figure 3.5).

Figure 3.5. Jobs created and destroyed, by gender, under ILO scenarios

Projections to 2030 (millions)

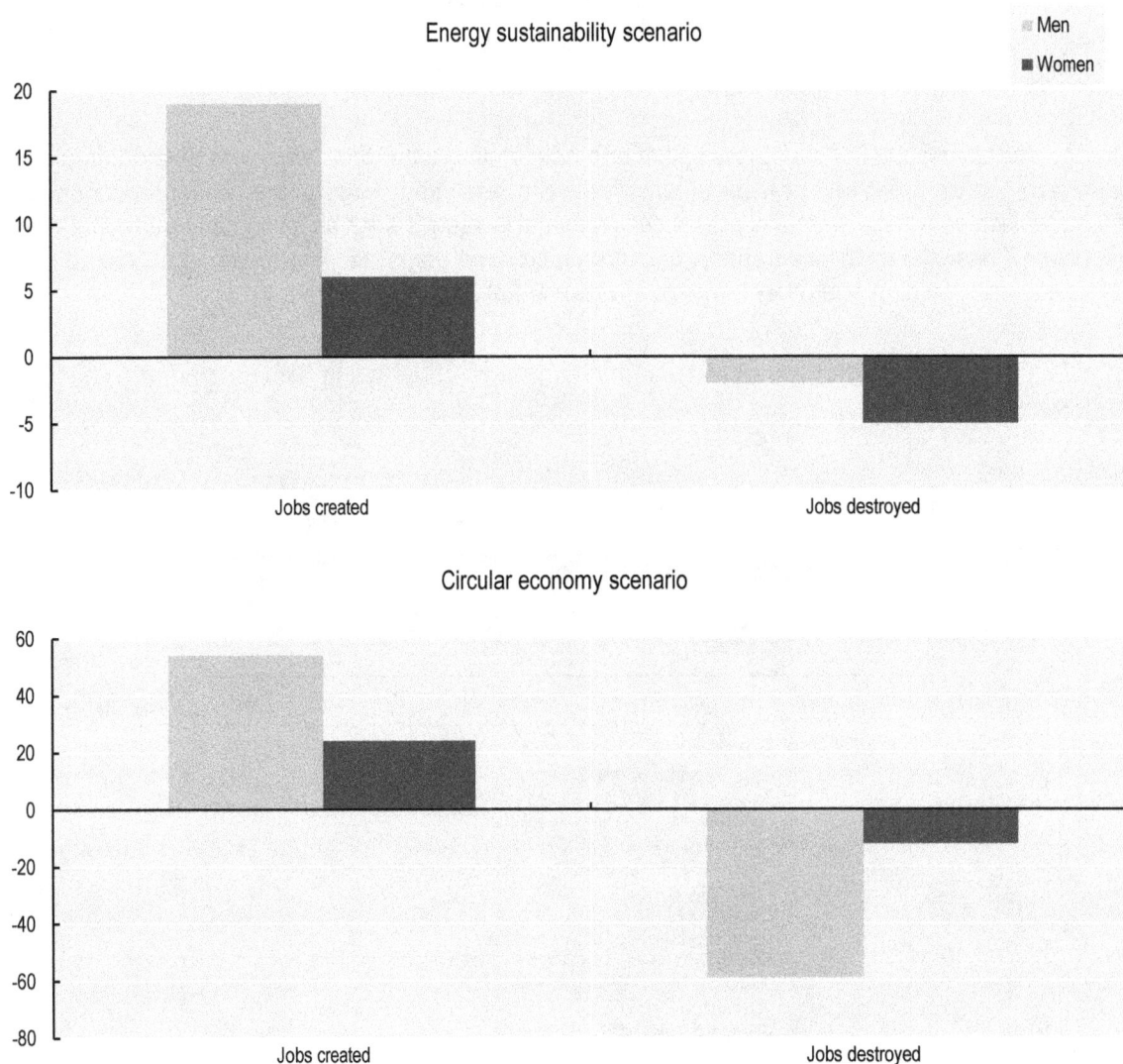

Note: ILO scenarios estimate job creation and job losses by 2030, based on data available for 32 countries, including the following OECD members: Australia, Costa Rica, Denmark, Estonia, France, Germany, Korea, Spain, United Kingdom and United States. The ILO energy sustainability scenario examines the changes in employment in the energy sector brought by the transition to energy sustainability (amount of energy produced and the way it is produced). The ILO circular economy scenario examines the changes in employment brought because of adopting circular modes of production and resource efficiency.
Source: (ILO, 2019[10]).

Based on limited gender-disaggregated data, the share of women in green occupations is low. In 2017 in France, for example, 82% of green occupations were held by men, compared to 52% for all occupations. Over-representation of men is particularly notable in sanitation and waste treatment technical professions. Women are more present in occupations that require high level qualifications, such as environmental engineering (Republique Française, 2020[11]).

Varying definitions of what constitutes environmental economic activity and green jobs (Box 3.2), which green skills may be required in the future, as well as a lack of available data, explain to a point countries' different approaches to the issue of developing green occupations and green skills for the transition to a green economy. These differences are also influenced by factors such as geography, income, education and social conditions, and may lead to gender inequalities and hamper women's economic empowerment.

> ### Box 3.2. Defining "green" jobs
>
> To date, there is no standard definition of "green economic activities" nor "green jobs". According to the ILO, "green jobs are decent jobs that contribute to preserve or restore the environment, be they in traditional sectors such as manufacturing and construction, or in new, emerging green sectors such as renewable energy and energy efficiency." They help to (i) improve energy and raw materials efficiency; (ii) limit greenhouse gas emissions; (iii) minimise waste and pollution; (iv) protect and restore ecosystems; and (v) support adaptation to the effects of climate change (ILO, n.d.[12]).
>
> Therefore, for ILO green jobs cover employment in production of environmental goods and services or employment in environmental friendly processes irrespective of economic activity, with the caveat that the jobs are also decent. In a European context, this means where quality employment and working conditions are guaranteed, with the aim of reducing inequalities and empowering people, especially women, youth and vulnerable groups (EC, n.d.[13]).
>
> In Mexico, the complementarities between the green and social economies are recognised. Therefore, green jobs are viewed with a specific focus on reducing inequalities and giving special attention to women's inclusion (ILO, 2013[14]).
>
> For data collection, the EU measures employment in the "environmental goods and services sector" (EGSS), which may exclude green jobs that are linked to the provision of goods and services for non- environmental purposes (Eurostat, 2009[15]).

Greece's GEAP includes general policy actions to increase women's labour force participation, but no measures specifically targeting environmental sectors or green jobs. Some of these measures are found in environment-related economic sectors[1] such as agriculture, but with no explicit link to environmental sustainability in their design Table 3.1. Some OECD members integrate gender considerations – most frequently focusing on education and the promotion of women's penetration in male-dominated industries – when developing green job incentives and policies in the framework of green growth. In some cases, countries apply tailored programmes to enhance women's labour access to environmental sectors (Box 3.2).

Table 3.2. Gender considerations taken into account in OECD countries' green job incentives and policies

	Funding for small business	Skills development/ capacity building	Education	Social measures to offset job displacement	Promotion of women in male-dominated industries	Other
Austria		•	•		•	
Belgium	•	•	•	•	•	
Costa Rica	•	•	•			
Estonia		•	•	•	•	
Germany					•	
Iceland					•	•
Ireland	•	•	•	•	•	
Latvia	•	•	•			•
Lithuania		•			•	
Luxembourg		•			•	
Slovenia	•					
Spain	•	•	•	•	•	
Sweden	•	•	•		•	•

Source: (OECD, 2020[16]).

To support women's economic empowerment in environmental sectors and green jobs, Greece could prioritise targeted vocational training and education, and encourage reskilling and upskilling for women already in the job market and those entering or re-entering. Advanced skills training for green occupations would support both women's labour participation and the transition to a green economy. Such initiatives could also be supported by specialised programmes for workers and workers with families that may require relocation, considering that new opportunities may no longer be available in the same geographical regions. Finally, guaranteeing overall gender balance in programmes may also increase women's participation and eventually entrance into the job market. This could be achieved by specific targeting in programme design, accompanied by outreach and awareness-raising.

A targeted approach to environment-related economic sectors with high levels of female participation could also be applied. In the case of agriculture, where a national policy framework already exists for women-led farmers' cooperatives (see section 2.3.3), promoting financial incentives (i.e. grants) to support women's participation in farming, and to increase women's knowledge and adoption of innovative farming techniques for sustainable agriculture should be considered. As seen in section 2.3.3, some EU member states have already introduced gender considerations in their programmes under the Common Agricultural Policy.

Box 3.3. Supporting women entrepreneurs in Chile

Chile's "Más Capaz Mujer Emprendedora" programme (see also Section 2.5.1). executed by the county's National Training and Employment Service (SENCE), helps women entrepreneurs maintain their presence in the market. The programme, which is already promoting female entrepreneurship in the artisanal fishing sector, is applicable to all economic sectors and provides knowledge on starting, improving and expanding a business. It offers women (i) 100 hours of training on managing and improving their business through design, evaluations and implementing a business model that responds to market opportunities; (ii) a Manual for Entrepreneurs, for starting their business; (iii) daily remuneration for transportation or food for attending the training programme; (iv) financial support at the end of the programme to start of strengthen their business venture; (v) financial support to mothers participating in the programme with children under the age of two; (vi) care facilities for children between two and 6 years old on the training site, or alternatively financial support to cover relevant expenses; and (vii) accident insurance for the beneficiary and the children for their transit to and from the training site.

In addition, Chile's Ministry of Women and Gender Equality, Ministry of Tourism and the national bank Banco Estado sponsor a "Tourist Businesswoman Contest" that awards winners with financing for their businesses. Contest conditions focus on sustainability, optimal use of natural resources, respect of socio-cultural authenticity of host communities and ensuring long-term viable economic development

Source: (Gobierno de Chile, n.d.[17]) (OECD, 2019[18]).

Women in eco-innovation

Engaging women in environmental innovation (eco-innovation) supports their representation in STEM-related fields and also could help drive the digital and green transitions. Greece's GEAP sets specific targets for increasing women's presence in innovation.

A Greek Innovation lab for Women (GIL4W) was recently established to provide support and promote research, innovation and entrepreneurship by and for women. GIL4W is a whole-of-government initiative in which 20 ministries, government agencies, research centres, and private sector stakeholders will participate. Priority will be given to strengthening women's presence in STEM fields in education, as well as in artificial intelligence and biotechnology. The initiative will also examine financing opportunities for woman-led business innovation initiatives (MoL, 2022[19]). To target women's further engagement in eco-innovation specifically, the GIL4W could consider introducing a "green" stream in its future programming, focusing on specific initiatives in environment-related male-dominated sectors.

Canada's "Science and Technology Internship Programme – Green Jobs" provided wage subsidies to eligible employers to hire and mentor youth in the natural resources sector, including in forestry, mining, earth science, and clean technology. The programme promotes equity, diversity and inclusion by targeting a 50% participation rate from non-represented groups, such as women, indigenous peoples, persons with disabilities and members of visible minorities. Results for 2017-2018 showed that 83% of the placements were in the clean technology sector, 53% of the employers were small and medium sized organisations, 63% of the youth participating also belonged in one of the employment equity groups, and 82% of the participants eventually found full-time employment (Government of Canada, n.d.[20]). Such programmes should also be considered by Greece, to support efforts in increasing women's inclusion in green innovation and other STEM-related green jobs.

Green skills

Identifying, assessing and creating green skills is essential in the transition to a low-carbon economy. Green skills are transversal; they cover the knowledge, abilities, values and attitudes needed to live in, develop and support a sustainable and resource-efficient society. Green skills are needed by the workforce in all sectors and at all levels in order adapt products, services and processes to climate change and to environmental requirements and regulations (OECD/Cedefop, 2014[21]). International and national commitments to achieving net zero by 2050 are already prompting government and industry initiatives for identifying green skills needed today and in the future.

The OECD describes green skills as "specific skills to modify products, services or operations due to climate change adjustments, requirements or regulations (e.g. water purification and site remediation planning/engineering in mining, solar panels installation, wind turbines design, green management, carbon capture and storage techniques)". They are considered converging skills, i.e. a combination of generic and high-knowledge-intensive skills (OECD, 2010[22]).

The United States' O*NET Resource Center, which maintains and updates occupational taxonomy, categorises green occupations into three groupings: (i) green enhanced skills occupations, whereby occupations remain the same even though tasks, skills, knowledge, credentials etc. are altered because of the impact of green economy activities and technologies; (ii) green increased demand occupations, whereby tasks remain the same but new positions are created due to increases in employment demand in sectors affected by the green transition; and (iii) green new and emerging occupations, whereby new occupations requiring new skills are unfolding as demands change. Within these caterories there are 183 occupations under 12 green economy sectors, with half being classified as green increased demand occupations (Dierdorff et al., 2015[23]).

The European Commission recently produced its own taxonomy for green skills. European Skills, Competences, Qualifications and Occupations (ESCO) covers 381 skills, 185 knowledge concepts and 5 transversal skills that are expected to be needed in the green transition. ESCO categorises skills as either (i) skills/competence concepts or (ii) knowledge concepts indicating the skill type (EC, 2022[24]). From the ESCO classification it is apparent that the green skills most in demand will be those linked to information; communication, collaboration and creativity; as well as assisting and caring. Prevailing green knowledge concepts are, by far, engineering, manufacturing and construction (Figure 3.6). All five transversal skills fall under the life skills and competences category (EC, 2022[24]).

As future green occupations are expected to include both existing and new tasks, it is imperative to strengthen women's training and knowledge around them. The United States National Bureau of Economic Research identifies four groups of tasks that are expected to be critical for green occupations: (i) engineering and technical skills, covering competences related to the design, construction and assessment of technology; (ii) science skills, linked to knowledge which can lead to innovation across the value chain; (iii) operation management skills, referring to skills necessary for introducing organisational change, life-cycle management, product development and sales; and (iv) monitoring skills, referring to non-technical skills necessary to comply with technical and legal standards (Vona et al., 2015[25]). The United Nations Industrial Development Organization (UNIDO) also specifies that soft skills related to design thinking, creativity, adaptability, resilience, are also considered as important for new jobs, including green jobs (Vidican Auktor, 2020[26]). Any training and skills development should therefore focus on motivating women to take up existing training for existing occupations that will be in high demand going forward, as well as reskilling and upskilling to cover new needs arising in the job market.

Figure 3.6. Green skills and knowledge concepts classification

ESCO taxonomy - January 2022

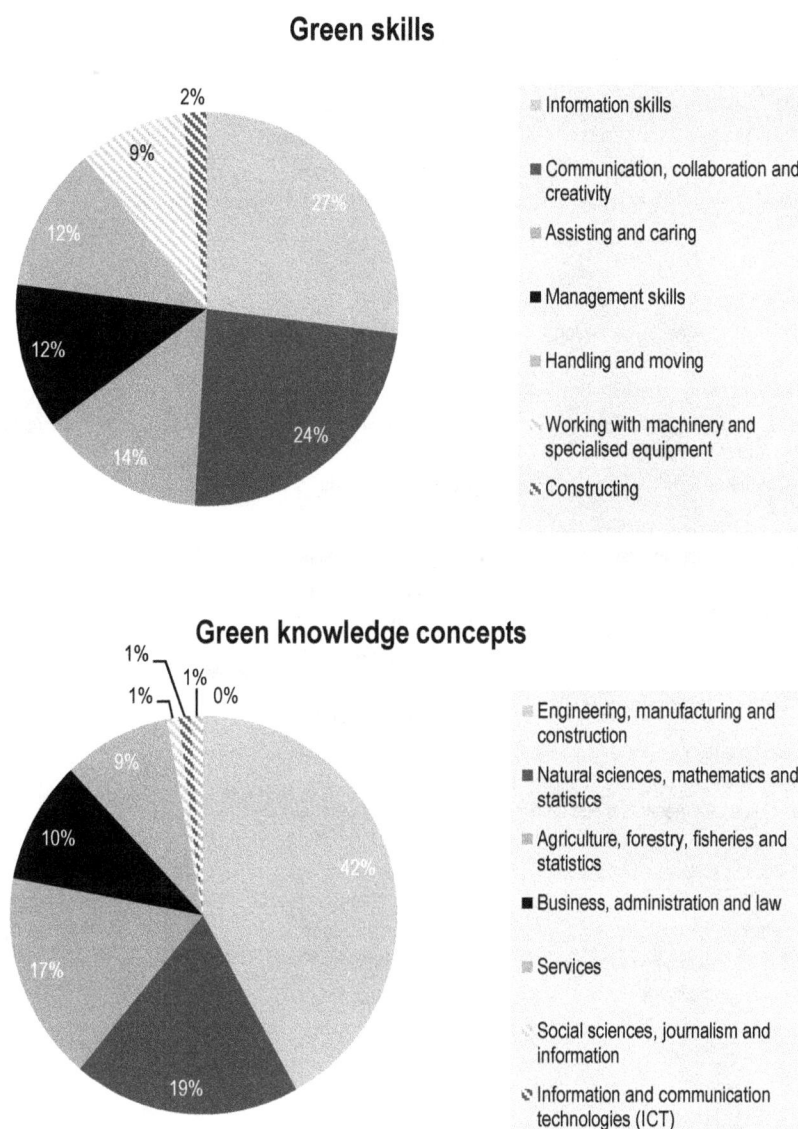

Green skills

Legend:
- Information skills
- Communication, collaboration and creativity
- Assisting and caring
- Management skills
- Handling and moving
- Working with machinery and specialised equipment
- Constructing

Values: 2%, 9%, 12%, 12%, 14%, 24%, 27%

Green knowledge concepts

Legend:
- Engineering, manufacturing and construction
- Natural sciences, mathematics and statistics
- Agriculture, forestry, fisheries and statistics
- Business, administration and law
- Services
- Social sciences, journalism and information
- Information and communication technologies (ICT)

Values: 1%, 1%, 1%, 0%, 9%, 10%, 17%, 19%, 42%

Note: CEDEFOP, the European Centre for the Development of Vocational Training, defines green skills and knowledge concepts as "knowledge, abilities, values and attitudes needed to live in, develop and support a society which reduces the impact of human activity on the environment." ESCO uses the same definition for classification.
Source: (EC, 2022[24])

In Greece, the Hellenic Federation of Enterprises (SEV) has identified 19 green occupations and 31 occupations that may require green skills and could contribute to the transition towards a green economy (Table 3.3). These occupations require knowledge of energy production, management and saving; technical skills on environmental impact assessment; knowledge on environmental risk management; digital skills to help monitor processes' efficiency, etc. (SEV, 2021[27]).

Table 3.3. Occupations in Greece that could contribute towards the green transition

Green occupations	Occupations where green skills may be required
Energy sector	
Specialised executive in Renewable Energy Sources technologies	Energy designer
Photovoltaic Systems Technician	Electricity systems specialised executive
Specialised executive in environmental protection issues	Energy investment advisor
Specialised executive in energy saving issues	Automation technician
Specialised executive in bioclimatic design & building applications	Specialised executive in automation issues
Wind systems technician	
Construction sector	
Specialised executive in environmental protection - Construction products' recycling	Specialised management executive for construction products quality
Construction engineer with energy specialisation	Specialised executive for construction products production
Sales & marketing executive for Energy efficient construction products (green marketing)	Construction products Research & Development executive
Bioclimatic buildings' architect	Construction products economy specialised executive
Metallurgy	
Environmental protection specialised executive - Metal products' recycling	Mining and mineral resources exploitation engineer
	Aluminium construction technician
	Equipment machinery operator
	Steel structures' craftsman
Environmental sector	*Logistics Sector*
Anti-pollution specialist	Logistics co-ordinator
Specialised executive in management and recycling of special waste (industrial etc.)	Supply chain manager
Responsible for water receivers monitoring and drinking water quality	Transportation manager
Industrial symbiosis advisor specialised on the environment	Logistics manager
Environmental economist	Distribution manager
Environmental auditing and certification specialist	Logistics engineer
Environmental application professions	Demand planner
Environmental lawyer	Purchasing/ Procurement manager
	Food sector
	Food safety & quality management executive
	Food marketing manager
	Scientific advisor to food companies
	R&D scientist
	Legal and communications officer
	Raw materials procurement manager
	Specialised food production executive
	Infrastructure & maintenance engineer
	Health sector
	Chemical engineer or chemist - specialised in pharmaceutical & parapharmaceutical research and production
	Medical auditor

Source: Author's compilation based on tables presented in (SEV, 2021[27]).

Skills policies are usually a horizontal endeavour covered by various government offices and organisations in OECD countries, including Greece, so inter-ministerial co-ordination and coherence is a necessity.

Introducing a green skills strategy at the national level, covering skills development and training from early education and to vocational training, could create a basis for better matching skills and environmental policies. In addition, securing a gender-responsive approach to a green skills policy framework would support women's economic empowerment and inclusion in growing green occupations.

Recently introduced legislation on upgrading workforce skills linked to the job market (Law 4921/2022) establishes a National Skills Council (NSC) tasked with preparing a skills strategy, following up on its implementation and coordinating actions between relevant bodies. The NSC is expected to prioritise developing a framework for digital skills. It will be supported by an experts' committee that will collect statistical data and advise the NSC on developing tools to upgrade skills for the Greek job market (OG, 2022[28]). As the Greek government is prioritising a digital and green transition under its recovery plan (see below), the NSC should include a specific section on green skills in its skills strategy.

Gender-sensitive green recovery in Greece

The ongoing COVID-19 and environmental crises have underscored the need to consider gender- and environment- responsive approaches to policy measures adopted by governments. Sustainable recovery measures that take inequalities into account could create opportunities for all and strengthen the system's resilience to future shocks. The OECD Green Recovery Database, is a tool set to help identify the likely environmental implications of the stimulus packages introduced (OECD, 2021[29]). A gender component is included to help identify gender-relevant and gender-sensitive measures. Latest data from the OECD Green Recovery Database show that only 2.5% of the policy measures introduced are gender relevant. These gender-relevant green recovery measures overwhelmingly have positive impacts on the environment in sectors such as buildings, energy, and surface transport. The majority of the gender-relevant measures contribute to supporting women's economic security, while also covering climate change mitigation and air pollution reduction as environmental targets (OECD, 2021[30]).

Greece is one of ten OECD countries with gender-sensitive green recovery policy measures. They are included in Greece's recovery and resilience plan and will be financially supported by the European Commission's Recovery and Resilience Facility. The three gender-sensitive policy measures, with a total budget of USD 557 million, focus on green skills and training in economic activities related to a circular economy. The programmes developed by the Greek Manpower Employment Organisation (OAED) do not include specific quotas for women's participation; however, women are the majority of participants in training programmes launched in recent years (Box 3.4).

Box 3.4. Training programmes for a green economy in Greece

The Greek Manpower Employment Organisation (OAED) is designing three training programmes to support the transition to a green economy. These programmes are financially supported by the EU's Recovery and Resilience Facility. The implementation is scheduled through national universities' Training and Life-Long Learning Centres.

Training in Smart and Sustainable Waste Management

The programme aims to provide training on pollution sources and waste management. Emphasis will be given to sustainable and smart urban development issues, through knowledge sharing on waste treatment efficiencies, reuse and recycling, in accordance to the national legal framework.

The programme targets secondary and higher education graduates interested in contributing to effective waste management. Moreover, employees in public environmental policy organisations,

---

environmental centres, as well as employees in local public environmental services, focusing on infrastructure, may also participate.

Organisation and Sustainability Principles for Agricultural Holdings

The purpose of the programme is to explain the economic, social, and environmental factors behind the viability of an agricultural holding, in light of challenges in agricultural products' competitiveness and digitalisation. The programme targets young and newcomer farmers (18-41 years of age), and will provide training on how to effectively manage their farm, and co-operate to gain easier and more efficient access to the market for their products.

The specific training programme includes subjects such as: (i) sustainability and competitiveness of agricultural holdings; (ii) increasing value added of agricultural products; (iii) conditions for sectoral and vertical integration of agricultural holdings; (iv) technical-economic parameters related to reducing production costs and increasing family income; (v) market-oriented small agricultural holdings; (vi) applying circular business models in agriculture; and (vii) developing digital skills and technologies.

2D and 3D Modelling and 3D Printing

This programme provides knowledge and training on designing and making toys from various environmentally friendly raw or reusable materials, as well as the material used (wood, biomaterials, resins, etc.). Specialised training on computer-aided design software for 2D and 3D modelling will also be provided, as well as opportunities for 3D printing. The programme is intended for both designers and professionals in producing products from raw materials, such as wood.

Source: Information provided by the Greek Manpower Employment Organisation (OAED)

3.2.2. Increasing women's participation in public life

Increasing women's participation in decision-making and leadership in the environmental public sector can lead to an increased focus on gender-specific environmental impacts and more effective environmental action (OECD, 2021[31]). Research suggests that a higher presence of women in decision-making positions in environment-related public positions may bring about more ambitious national climate goals and policies (Strumskyte, Ramos Magaña and Bendig, 2022[32]). OECD member countries appear to consider female representation as a key component for environmental sustainability. In fact, 39% of all OECD environment ministers were women in 2021 (Strumskyte, Ramos Magaña and Bendig, 2022[32]).

Several OECD members apply measures to achieve gender balance in environmental decision-making in the public sector, with representation in key leadership positions and management boards of public entities being those mostly applied (Table 3.4).

Table 3.4. Measures applied by OECD members to ensure or track gender balance in decision-making in environmental policies and sectors

	Measures for gender-balance in:				
	Key environmental leadership positions	Senior management at the environment authority	Delegations to national or international environment-related events	Management or boards of public entities in environmental sectors	Public consultations
Austria	•	•	•	•	
Belgium	•	•	•	•	•
Colombia	•	•	•	•	•

	Measures for gender-balance in:				
	Key environmental leadership positions	Senior management at the environment authority	Delegations to national or international environment-related events	Management or boards of public entities in environmental sectors	Public consultations
Denmark				•	
Estonia		•			
Germany	•	•	•	•	•
Greece	•	•	•	•	•
Iceland	•	•		•	
Ireland	•	•	•	•	•
Japan	•	•	•	•	
Latvia	•				
Lithuania			•		•
Luxembourg	•	•	•	•	•
Mexico	•	•	•	•	•
Netherlands	•	•	•	•	•
Norway	•	•	•	•	•
Slovenia	•		•	•	•
Spain	•	•	•	•	•
Sweden	•	•	•	•	•

Source: (OECD, 2020[16])

Systematically pursuing women's participation in leadership and decision-making environmental positions in public life, as well as guaranteeing gender balance in senior positions, would help to minimise gender gaps. Many OECD countries, including Greece, apply horizontal initiatives for the whole policy spectrum. Greece has introduced a one-third rule for all public administration bodies, whereby both sexes must represent at least one-third of membership, unless the composition is based on positions and not related tasks (Law 2839/2000). Therefore, gender balance is not always achieved.

Greece has introduced a 25% quota for women in management board membership of listed companies, as well as diversity principles based on non-discrimination. National bodies and committees apply gender quotas, but there is still no systematic pursue of women's participation in leadership and decision-making positions in environment-related public bodies. This also applies to representation at international environmental negotiations, such as the UNFCCC COPs, where Greece is the OECD member with the widest variability in women's participation, indicating that there has not been a consistent political decision on gender balance in its national delegation (Figure 3.7).

Figure 3.7. Women's participation as country representatives in UNFCCC Conferences of the Parties (COPs)

OECD countries - 2019 data

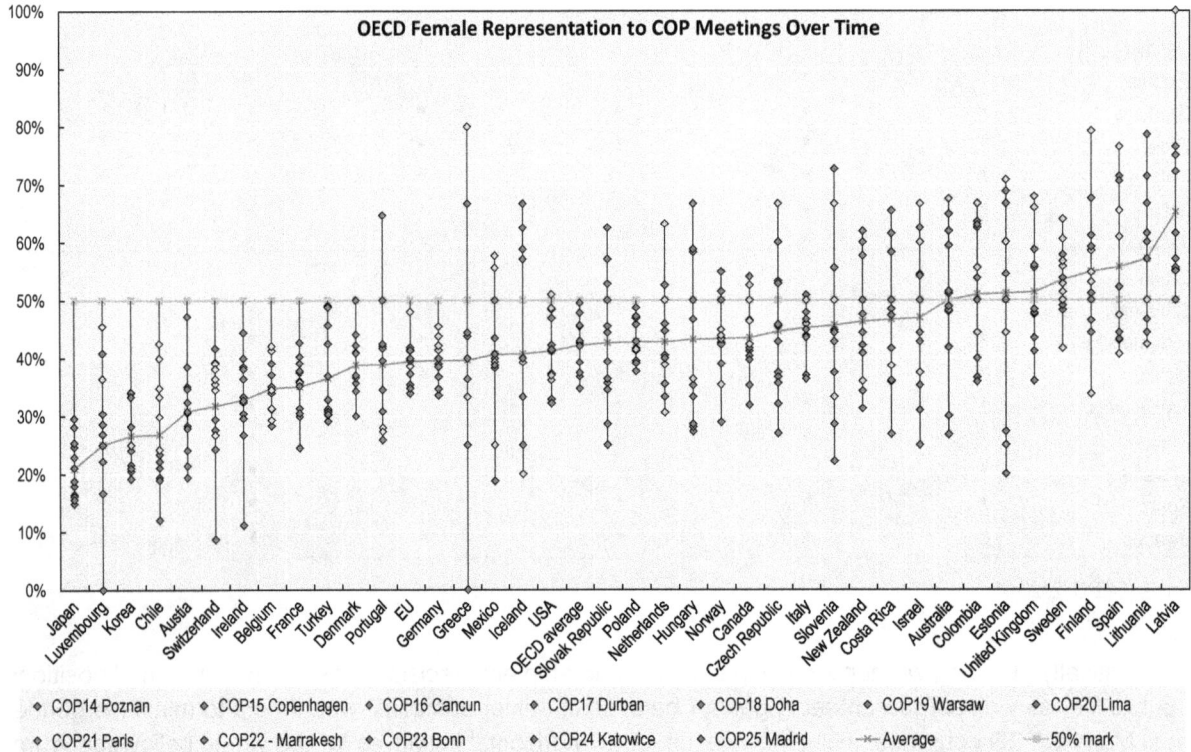

Note: Women's participation in the annual Conference of the Parties to the UN Framework Convention on Climate Change (COP) for the period 2008-2019, as a percentage of the total size of the national delegation. Yellow diamonds indicate that a woman was heading the delegation. The red line projects the average value per country.
Source: (OECD, 2021[31])

3.2.3. Combatting gender-based violence

Greece's GEAP attaches a high priority to combatting gender-based and domestic violence, especially since the country ratified the Istanbul Convention in 2018. Gender-based violence is expected to have increased during the COVID-19 lockdown period (MoL, 2021[7]). The GEAP covers prevention, protection and recovery measures on gender-based violence against women and girls (GBVAWG), but does not identify interlinkages between gender-based violence and sectoral policies such as urban planning and transportation.

Uncontrolled urbanisation around the world has led to limited housing access, densification and air quality degradation, compromising cities' overall well-being and sustainability. Air and noise pollution and urban densification has been associated with stress, anxiety, depression and other mental health conditions (Kioumourtzoglou et al., 2017[33]). Studies in US cities have found a correlation between pollution and violent behaviours and crime, which have the potential to increase GBVAWG (Burkhardt et al., 2019[34]). Conversely, environmental quality, including access to green areas and physical activity, is increasingly recognised for its role in improving well-being, quality of life and mental health. Enhancing well-being through access to blue and green spaces could be part of a holistic policy approach to curtailing GBVAWG.

3.2.4. Mainstreaming gender in sectoral policies

Statistics to support gender mainstreaming in environmental policies

Designing gender-sensitive and gender-responsive policies requires, first and foremost, appropriate statistical data and indicators in order to identify gaps in policy making and monitor policy implementation.

The gender-environment nexus is not frequently observed in data collection efforts among OECD member countries. The gender-disaggregated and gender-relevant data that is collected is usually on labour participation, gender pay gaps, demographic data etc. More information in relation to environmental and environment-related sectors, climate change and environmental health would allow for a more granular approach when applying the gender-environment nexus.

Based on a 2019 OECD Survey, only 11 member countries confirmed collecting gender-disaggregated data related to environmental policies. Among these countries, the data/information is non-homogenous, ranging from use practices to exposure or workforce participation in environmental and environment-related economic activities, or green jobs. Greece's survey response indicated that it does not collect any gender-disaggregated environmental data (OECD, 2019[35]). Yet, a much larger number of OECD members declared that they do consider gender aspects in environmental policy making, albeit not always in a systematic way. This is done, for example, when applying gender impact assessments or risk assessments that incorporate gender considerations in environmental policy making, or gender considerations in budgeting for environment (OECD, 2020[16]). The disconnect between gender-disaggregated data collected and the gender considerations integrated in environmental policy making shows there is still room for improvement to better mainstream gender in this policy area.

OECD countries such as Estonia, Finland, France, Iceland, Sweden and the United Kingdom collect gender-disaggregated information on attitudes, perceptions and behaviour related to environmental issues through sectoral surveys (e.g. on mobility, consumption patterns, recycling and waste management) (OECD, 2020[16]).

Box 3.5. Sweden's gender-disaggregated data collection around environment-related policies

Statistics Sweden, the country's statistical agency, has developed gender equality indicators and collects gender-disaggregated data as part implementation of Sweden's 1993 gender equality strategy.

Land use statistics include ownership by gender. Gender-disaggregated data is also collected for environmental economic accounts on the environmental goods and services sector and on bio-economy. In addition, Sweden collects data relating to environmental health, such as on noise exposure, air quality, time spent in green spaces, or even exposure to food contaminants and agricultural chemicals exposure.

Sweden's Consumer Agency collects information on consumer perceptions and attitudes, not only disaggregated by gender but also correlated to income, which shows different consumption patterns in sectors such as transport, food and used goods.

Source: (OECD, 2020[16]); (OECD, 2019[36]).

Greece does collect statistical data around the environment, but improvements could be made, especially in relation to waste statistics, circular economy, and monitoring employment trends and labour reallocation due to shrinking and growing activities (OECD, 2020[37]). Greece is one of the few EU member states that does not collect data on employment in the environmental goods and services (EGSS) sector.

Greece's GEAP urges each ministry to integrate a gender dimension in their public policies; including setting annual targets, adopting indicators and producing gender impact assessment reports for upcoming legislation. This approach, if implemented by the public administration working on environment, climate change, energy and other environment-related policy fields, in collaboration with the Hellenic Statistical Authority and the GSDFPGE, would support gender mainstreaming and better environmental policy making. This may require additional capacity development, especially in cases where multiple factors, and not only gender, intersect and may lead to differentiated environmental impacts for policies by gender.

Gender budgeting and financing

Some OECD members have introduced gender considerations in their national budget preparations through impact assessments, resource allocation and performance setting (OECD, 2018[38]). However, when asked whether gender considerations are taken into account when creating budgets related to environmental policy, only four OECD countries replied they always do (Figure 3.8).

Figure 3.8. Gender considerations in budgeting relating to environmental policies

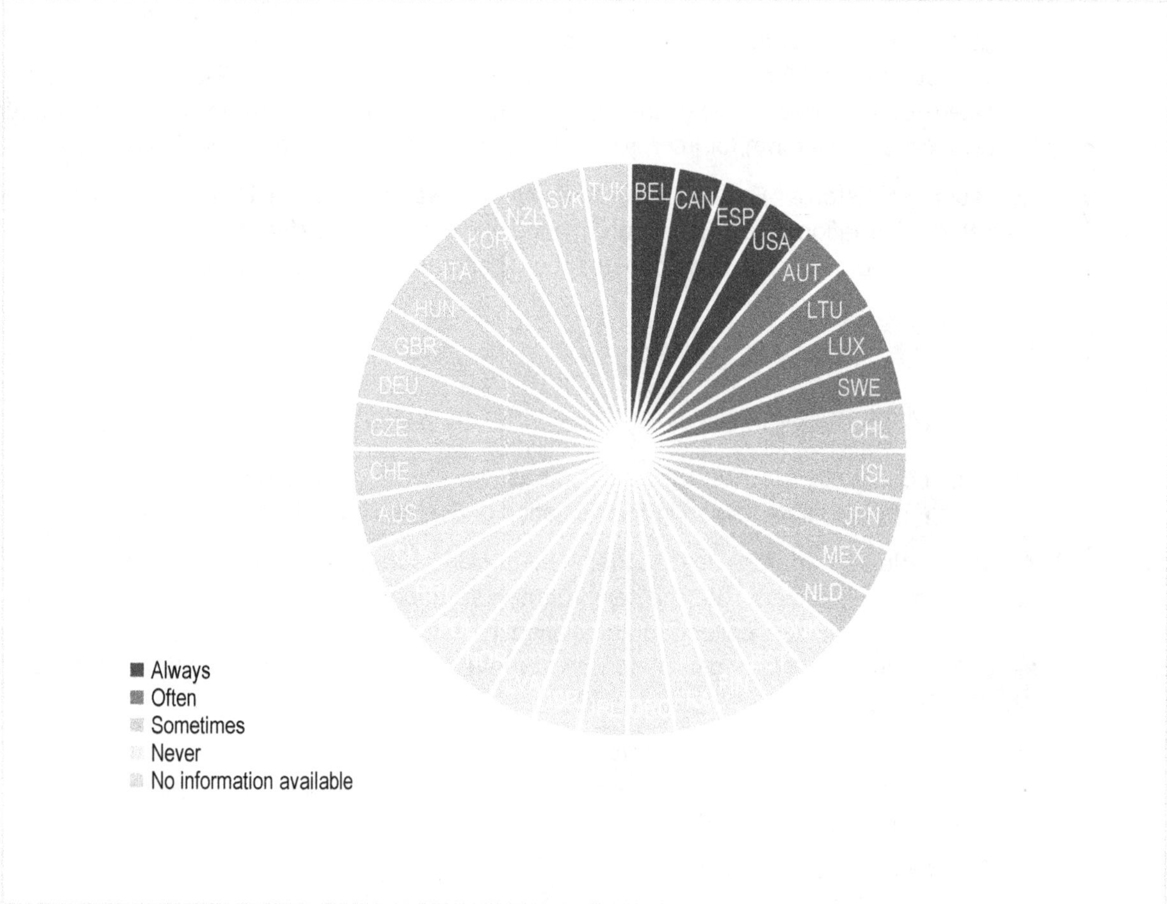

Source: (OECD, 2020[16]).

In Belgium, each government department, agency and state-owned enterprise incorporates a gender analysis for projects financed by the national budget (OECD, 2019[39]). Canada has committed from 2018 to take into consideration the impacts of policies on all Canadians in a budgetary content (OECD, 2019[40]). In Spain, all ministries are requested to include a gender impact report analysing the gender impact of their spending programmes; a provision which also applies to the Ministry of Ecological Transition. The programmes are aligned with the objectives of Spain's national Strategic Plan for Equal Opportunities, as well as thematic or sectoral equality plans, which allows to carry out an identification of planned actions, as well as a very specific diagnosis for each spending programme (OECD, 2019[41]).

Governments are also using environmentally responsive or "green budgeting" as a way to record and communicate policy progress on environmental policy objectives through budgeting processes. Integrating gender and green principles and criteria in budgeting processes in a coherent manner could leverage efforts towards a more sustainable and inclusive budgeting framework.

Only a handful of OECD countries measure gender impacts of state subsidies in environment-related sectors. For instance, Finland's Ministry of Agriculture and Forestry conducts an *ex-ante* gender impact evaluation of agricultural subsidies for the country's Rural Development Programme. It then uses the assessment's outcomes to crosscheck the subsidy's compatibility with the national Equality Act. Sweden, on the other hand, conducts *ex-post* analysis on the impact and effect of an applicant's gender on agricultural subsidies. In Spain, there is a mandatory provision for gender analysis on all subsidies, however, in most cases, no gender equality impacts are identified (OECD, 2020[16]).

Beyond state budgeting, integrating the gender-environment nexus into project programming and investment planning could support the shift to a more inclusive and green economy. Capital budget proposals for infrastructure investments should include gender and environment impact assessments to cover non-monetised impacts to standard cost-benefit analysis (OECD, forthcoming[42]).

Mainstreaming gender through public consultations

Greece requires public consultation on all draft primary laws. There is no such obligation for secondary draft legislation, which supports the implementation of primary laws (OECD, 2021[43]). With regards to disseminating environmental information and including public consultation, Greece has a guaranteed legal framework and has also enhanced its effectiveness, using online tools. More active public participation would be welcome, and would require dedicating more resources to data collection, classification and management (OECD, 2020[37]).

Women's organisations and other gender equality stakeholders could contribute to public consultations by emphasising the positive impacts of environmental policy on gender equality and women's empowerment. To increase their participation, public administration could provide more detailed analysis on possible differentiated impacts of proposed legislation or other initiatives under public consultation from an early stage through drafting, going beyond what is usually included under regulatory impact assessments (OECD, 2021[44]). Greece includes gender-related questions in its Regulatory Impact Assessment for every primary draft law submitted to Parliament; however, lack of data or even a gender-blind approach may lead to leaving the information blank. A more active representation of civil society's perspective on gender equality in public consultations would bring forward these issues (as the public consultations' results are attached to the RIA submitted to Parliament).

In addition, gender balance in public bodies that actively provide input to line ministries could also bring to the forefront other issues and priorities. In the case of environmental and climate policy, women's leadership in environmental public governance could translate into more ambitions climate goals and could influence environmental and climate policies, and negotiations (Strumskyte, Ramos Magaña and Bendig, 2022[32]). Guaranteeing women's participation in bodies such as the National Observatory for Circular Economy, the National Observatory for Climate Change Adaptation and the relevant scientific and stakeholder committees could therefore lead to better policy outcomes on both gender equality and environmental sustainability.

References

Burkhardt, J. et al. (2019), "The effect of pollution on crime: Evidence from data on particulate matter and ozone", *Journal of Environmental Economics and Management*, Vol. 98, p. 102267, https://doi.org/10.1016/j.jeem.2019.102267. [34]

Commission, E. (ed.) (n.d.), *Employment and decent work*, https://www.ilo.org/global/topics/green-jobs/news/WCMS_220248/lang--en/index.htm (accessed on 20 January 2022). [13]

Dierdorff, E. et al. (2015), *Greening of the World of Work: Revisiting Occupational Consequences*. [23]

EC (2022), *Green skills and knowledge concepts: Labelling the ESCO classification - Technical Report*, https://esco.ec.europa.eu/system/files/2022-03/Green%20Skills%20and%20Knowledge%20-%20Labelling%20ESCO_0.pdf (accessed on 25 May 2022). [24]

EIGE (2021), *Gender Equality Index*, https://eige.europa.eu/gender-equality-index/2021/country/EL. [3]

Eurostat (2009), *The environmental goods and services sector - A data collection handbook*, Office for Official Publications of the European Communities, https://doi.org/10.2785/31117. [15]

Gil, B., A. Sánchez López and L. Murillo (2013), *Green jobs and related policy frameworks - An overview of the European Union*. [9]

Gobierno de Chile (n.d.), *+Capaz Mujer Emprendedora: El programa de capacitación para mujeres que quieren empezar o mejorar su negocio*, https://www.gob.cl/noticias/capaz-mujer-emprendedora-el-programa-de-capacitacion-para-mujeres-que-quieren-empezar-o-mejorar-su-negocio/#:~:text=%C2%BFQu%C3%A9%20es%20el%20programa%20%2BCapaz,poner%20en%20marcha%20un%20negocio. [17]

Government of Canada (n.d.), *Green jobs in natural resources*, https://www.nrcan.gc.ca/climate-change-adapting-impacts-and-reducing-emissions/canadas-green-future/green-jobs/87 (accessed on 14 February 2022). [20]

ILO (2019), *Skills for a greener future: A global view based on 32 country studies*, https://www.ilo.org/wcmsp5/groups/public/---ed_emp/documents/publication/wcms_732214.pdf. [10]

ILO (2013), *Evaluation of the potential of green jobs in Mexico*, https://www.ilo.org/wcmsp5/groups/public/@ed_emp/@emp_ent/documents/publication/wcms_236143.pdf. [14]

ILO (n.d.), *What is a green job?*, https://www.ilo.org/global/topics/green-jobs/news/WCMS_220248/lang--en/index.htm (accessed on 20 January 2022). [12]

Kioumourtzoglou, M. et al. (2017), "The Association Between Air Pollution and Onset of Depression Among Middle-Aged and Older Women", *American Journal of Epidemiology*, Vol. 185/9, pp. 801-809, https://doi.org/10.1093/aje/kww163. [33]

Kourtali, E. (2021), *DZ Bank: Ομόλογα ύψους 16 δισ. ερυώ θα εκδώσει η Ελλάδα το 2022 - Το...* [45]
ρεκόρ με το πράσινο ομόλογο, https://www.capital.gr/agores/3593576/dz-bank-omologa-upsous-16-dis-tha-ekdosei-i-ellada-to-2022-to-rekor-me-to-prasino-omologo (accessed on 15 March 2022).

MoL (2022), *Ξεκινάει τη λειτουργία του το «Κέντρο Καινοτομίας για τις Γυναίκες»*, [19]
https://ypergasias.gov.gr/xekinaei-ti-leitourgia-tou-to-kentro-kainotomias-gia-tis-gynaikes/ (accessed on 13 February 2022).

MoL (2021), *Εθνικό Σχέδιο Δράσης για την Ισότητα των Φύλων 2021-2025*, [7]
https://isotita.gr/esdif-2021-2025/.

OECD (2022), *Labour force participation rate* (indicator), https://doi.org/10.1787/8a801325-en [8]
(accessed on 3 May 2022).

OECD (2021), *Gender and the Environment: Building Evidence and Policies to Achieve the* [31]
SDGs, OECD Publishing, Paris, https://doi.org/10.1787/3d32ca39-en.

OECD (2021), "Gender-relevance of policies in the OECD Green Recovery Database", *OECD* [30]
Policy Responses to Coronavirus (COVID-19), OECD Publishing, Paris,
https://doi.org/10.1787/e6a03378-en.

OECD (2021), *OECD Regulatory Policy Outlook 2021*, OECD Publishing, Paris, [43]
https://doi.org/10.1787/38b0fdb1-en.

OECD (2021), *Policy framework for gender-sensitive public governance - Meeting of the Council* [44]
at Ministerial Level, 5-6 October 2021, https://www.oecd.org/mcm/Policy-Framework-for-Gender-Sensitive-Public-Governance.pdf.

OECD (2021), "The OECD Green Recovery Database: Examining the environmental [29]
implications of COVID-19 recovery policies", *OECD Policy Responses to Coronavirus*
(COVID-19), OECD Publishing, Paris, https://doi.org/10.1787/47ae0f0d-en.

OECD (2020), *EPOC Survey on integrating gender in environmental policies*. [16]

OECD (2020), *OECD Environmental Performance Reviews: Greece 2020*, OECD Environmental [37]
Performance Reviews, OECD Publishing, Paris, https://doi.org/10.1787/cec20289-en.

OECD (2019), *EPOC Survey on integrating gender in environmental policies - Belgium's* [39]
response.

OECD (2019), *EPOC Survey on integrating gender in environmental policies - Canada's* [40]
response.

OECD (2019), *EPOC Survey on integrating gender in environmental policies - Chile's response*. [18]

OECD (2019), *EPOC Survey on integrating gender in environmental policies - Greece's* [35]
response.

OECD (2019), *EPOC Survey on integrating gender in environmental policies - Spain's response*. [41]

OECD (2019), *EPOC Survey on integrating gender in environmental policies - Sweden's* [36]
response.

OECD (2019), *SIGI 2019 Global Report: Transforming Challenges into Opportunities*, Social [4]
Institutions and Gender Index, OECD Publishing, Paris, https://doi.org/10.1787/bc56d212-en.

OECD (2019), *SIGI Policy Simulator*, [6]
https://sim.oecd.org/Default.ashx?lang=En&ds=SIGI&d1c=oecd&d2c=grc&cs=eur (accessed
on 25 January 2022).

OECD (2018), *2018 International Budget Practices and Procedures Database*, [38]
https://qdd.oecd.org/subject.aspx?Subject=BPP_2018 (accessed on 25 March 2022).

OECD (2017), *2013 OECD Recommendation of the Council on Gender Equality in Education,* [47]
Employment and Entrepreneurship, OECD Publishing, Paris,
https://doi.org/10.1787/9789264279391-en.

OECD (2010), *SMEs, Entrepreneurship and Innovation*, OECD Studies on SMEs and [22]
Entrepreneurship, OECD Publishing, Paris, https://doi.org/10.1787/9789264080355-en.

OECD (n.d.), *OECD Gender Portal*, https://www.oecd.org/gender/ (accessed on 15 May 2022). [5]

OECD (forthcoming), *Supporting women's empowerment through green policies and finance.* [42]

OECD/Cedefop (2014), *Greener Skills and Jobs*, OECD Green Growth Studies, OECD [21]
Publishing, Paris, https://doi.org/10.1787/9789264208704-en.

OG (2022), *Law 4921/2022 - Δουλειές Ξανά: Αναδιοργάνωση Δημόσιας Υπηρεσίας* [28]
Απασχόλησης και ψηφιοποίηση των υπηρεσιών της, αναβάθμιση δεξιοτήτων εργατικού
δυναμικού και διοργάνωσης των αναγκών εργασίας και άλλες διατάξεις, Official Government
Gazette.

OG (2022), *Law 4936/2022 - Εθνικός Κλιματικός Νόμος - Μετάβαση στην κλιματική ουδετερότητα* [46]
και προσαρμογή στην κλιματική αλλαγή, επείγουσες διατάξεις για την αντιμετώπιση της
ενεργειακής κρίσης και την προστασία του περιβάλλοντος, Official Government Gazette.

Republique Française (2020), *Part des femmes dans les professions vertes en 2017 (en%)*, [11]
https://www.notre-environnement.gouv.fr/donnees-et-
ressources/ressources/graphiques/article/part-des-femmes-dans-les-professions-vertes-en-
2014-en (accessed on 15 May 2022).

SEV (2021), *Πράσινη οικονομία και απασχόληση: προκλήσεις και προτάσεις για μια δίκαιη* [27]
μετάβαση, https://www.sev.org.gr/wp-
content/uploads/2021/07/SR_GREEN_JOBS_V18_FINAL.pdf (accessed on
15 September 2021).

Strumskyte, S., S. Ramos Magaña and H. Bendig (2022), "Women's leadership in environmental [32]
action", *OECD Environment Working Papers*, No. 193, OECD Publishing, Paris,
https://doi.org/10.1787/f0038d22-en.

Vidican Auktor, G. (2020), *Green industrial skills for a sustainable future*, [26]
https://lkdfacility.org/wp-content/uploads/LKDForum-2020_Green-Skills-for-a-Sustainable-
Future.pdf.

Vona, F. et al. (2015), *Green skills*, http://www.nber.org/papers/w21116 (accessed on [25]
15 February 2022).

World Bank (2022), *Women, Business and the Law*, The World Bank, https://doi.org/10.1596/978-1-4648-1817-2. [1]

World Bank (2022), *World, Business and the Law*, https://wbl.worldbank.org/en/wbl (accessed on 28 April 2022). [2]

Notes

[1] As noted in previous chapters, environmental sectors are economic sectors that generate environmental products, such as goods and services produced for environmental protection or resource management. The term environment-related economic sectors and activities is broader and covers other economic sectors and activities that may have an environmental impact.

4 Recommendations for better integrating the gender-environment nexus into policies in Greece

This chapter presents recommendations for how to better integrate the gender-environment nexus into Greece's policy framework, focussing on actions that require co-operation and engagement of multiple stakeholders.

Integrating the gender-environment nexus into national policies requires tools and initiatives that mainstream gender in sectoral policies and enhance women's role in the economy and society. This chapter proposes thirty recommendations, under five targets, that could be explored and adopted by Greece. They are intended to complement Greece's Gender Equality Action Plan (GEAP) by applying an environmental lens to the Plan's main goals of achieving women's economic empowerment; supporting women's presence in leadership and decision making; raising women's voices on environment-related issues through environmental justice; and mainstreaming gender in environmental policies (see also Table 3.1).

The following targets and recommendations were prepared in the context of this report for Greece, but could be useful for other countries wishing to integrate the gender-environment nexus into their national policies.

4.1. Target 1. Gender mainstreaming in environmental and climate policies

Develop and apply gender-responsive and gender-sensitive environmental policy tools.

- Assess environmental and climate policies, strategies and actions to identify their gender-differentiated impacts. Gender implications may be related to broader social impacts, cost issues, or localised effects for specific population groups who may be more vulnerable to the effects of certain measures (Chapter 2).
- Reinforce the Greek Action Plan on Green Public Procurement with gender-sensitive initiatives in order to stimulate better environmental and social performance of products and services purchased (section 2.5.2).
  - Expand capacity assessments to include both environmental and gender equality standards.
  - Produce guidelines to support the coexistence of gender equality and environmental sustainability in public procurement.
  - Collect data on enterprises led by women, enterprises that apply gender equality standards, and enterprises that apply environmental standards and circular business models.
  - Evaluate the gender equity and environmental impact of bids through consultation with other public authorities and civil society to develop the public procurement process in a more gender-neutral and environmentally sustainable manner.
  - Advance socio-economic goals through procurements, for example by purchasing from small businesses and businesses led by or that mainly employ women.
- Follow the proposed framework set out in the OECD's Selected stocktaking of good practices for inclusion of women in infrastructure (OECD, 2021[1]) (section 2.3.2), specifically:
  - long-term vision for gender-responsive infrastructure;
  - women's voice and agency in infrastructure decision-making;
  - gender considerations in project appraisal, selection, risk assessment and design;
  - gender-sensitive infrastructure procurement and delivery;
  - gender angle in monitoring and evaluation.

4.2. Target 2. Women's economic empowerment in male-dominated environmental sectors

Overcome gender stereotypes, cultural beliefs and implicit biases that create obstacles for women and girls in environment-related economic activities. Increase women's presence in male-dominated environmental sectors, and acknowledge women's existing participation in green economic activities.

4.2.1. Women and green innovation

- Support women and girls' future inclusion in environmental economic activities by further developing the Green Innovation Lab for Women or introducing complementary measures. Foster girls' stronger engagement in STEM subjects and educational programmes that develop environmental knowledge and skills. This approach requires not only a high uptake from women and girls, but also from educators, career counsellors, research agencies, and their families (sections 2.4 and 3.2.1).

- Provide targeted assistance (financial or other) to support women's STEM-related entrepreneurial activity with a view towards environmental and environment-related economic activities or climate action (sections 2.4 and 2.5.1).

- Increase women's inclusion in green technology and eco-innovation by continuing to encourage their participation in artificial intelligence (Table 3.1), and more actions and resources to promote programmes that improve the uptake of women's scientific research and innovation (section 3.2.1).

- Introduce a "green stream" in the future programming of the Greek Innovation Lab for Women, with specific initiatives in environment-related male-dominated sectors (section 3.2.1).

4.2.2. Women in green jobs

- Develop a national green skills strategy through inter-ministerial co-ordination. Map occupations and skills needed to support the transition to a green economy. Analyse skills development by gender, covering both "traditional" and "generic" green skills, taking into account the existing employment gap in environment-related sectors (sections 2.5.1 and 3.2.1).

- Ensure that upskilling, reskilling and other training is inclusive and open not only to workers facing unemployment or relocation due to climate change mitigation policies, but also to women who wish to enter the green job market (section 2.2.2).

- Introduce mentoring programmes for women and girls specifically in green jobs, in collaboration with the private sector (section 2.5.1).

- Further enhance gender-sensitive agriculture and forestry policies to increase women's participation in the sector. Acknowledge women's role in agriculture and farming. Record women's formal and informal participation in sustainable agriculture and farming. Link social security benefits and public financing opportunities to better reflect women's contribution in agriculture and rural development. Further support women farmers and women-led agricultural co-operatives that use traditional knowledge and prioritise organic farming, agro-tourism and sustainable agricultural practices (innovation). Increase women's knowledge and adoption of innovative farming techniques (sections 2.3.3 and 3.2.1).

4.2.3. Women and green entrepreneurship

- Further promote learning and coaching programmes to help women entrepreneurs start or reshape green businesses, including education on circular economy business models and financial planning (section 2.5.1).

- Develop financial incentives for women-owned green businesses related to circular economy activities or business models. This could also include incentives to promote product service system models (section 2.5.1).

- Support women entrepreneurs struggling to maintain their presence in the green economy, including through financial support to assist with personal/family responsibilities (unpaid care work) (section 2.5.1).

- Further support the participation of women-led co-operatives in auctions for renewable energy production (wind and solar) through incentives such as lower tariffs for small developers (section 2.2.2).

4.3. Target 3. Women's presence in environmental leadership and decision making

- Analyse and pursue gender parity in decision-making bodies related to environmental planning (e.g. the National Observatory for Climate Change Adaptation and the National Circular Economy Observatory), finance, and budgeting, as well as in representation at international, national and local environmental negotiations (sections 2.5.4, 3.2.2).

- Systematically pursue gender balance in multi-level governance mechanisms and advisory bodies (e.g. as currently done in the National Council for Research, Technology and Innovation, and the Natural Environment and Climate Change Agency Management Board) by including stakeholders from public authorities, regional and local governments, the private sector and academia. Support better representation of women in the discussion and design of financial and other incentives for achieving environmental and climate targets (sections 2.5.4 and 3.2.4).

- Enhance women's representation and leadership in environment-related economic sectors (e.g. related to the circular economy). Introduce awards or other incentives for women participating in environmental leadership and decision-making, or eco-innovation, to recognise their contributions and incentivise more women to enter these fields (section 2.5.4).

- Guarantee/promote greater diversity in clean energy professions through career development initiatives (engage all stakeholders – public administration, private sector, and academia). Foster women's return to the workforce or restarting their careers (section 2.4).

4.4. Target 4. Gender-sensitive environmental justice

- Present new environmental and climate legislation or policy measures in a gender-sensitive manner, in order to incite interest from the public and women-led organisations and civil society (sections 2.3.1, 2.3.2, and 2.5.1).

- Include gender equality advocates in public consultations for environmental and climate policies. Promote gender justice by explicitly involving women as co-creators, making them visible and heard and empowering them to design, manage and take ownership of their living environments (sections 2.3.2, 2.5.2, 2.6 and 3.2.4).

- Evaluate women's equal access to environmental justice through collecting data on their access to environmental information, participation in public consultations on environmentally sensitive projects and infrastructure development, and community engagement (section 3.2.4).

4.4.1. Highlight women's green behaviour

- Inform and educate consumers on sustainable consumption, taking into account women's and men's differentiated preferences around household consumption, waste generation and prevention (sections 2.5.3, and 3.2.4).
- Integrate a gender-sensitive approach in awareness raising around environmental issues, energy saving and energy efficiency policies. Adapt messaging when designing effective public communication campaigns on sustainable household consumption and on promoting eco-labelling (section 2.2.1).
- Incentivise reducing municipal waste, which at household level are usually the responsibility of women, by providing financial and other incentives, such as access to other municipal services (childcare services, public transport access and use, etc.) (section 2.5.3).
- Introduce gender-sensitive urban planning and mobility by considering women's needs, travel preferences and mobility patterns (section 2.3.1).

4.5. Target 5. Statistical data and monitoring progress on integrating the gender-environment nexus

Greece should build up its statistical data and develop indicators to observe and monitor progress on integrating the gender-environment nexus in its overall policy framework. Overcoming the current lack of available data and indicators would facilitate aligning and capitalising on the interlinkages between gender-equality and environmental policies.

- Collect data on the environmental goods and services sector and sex-disaggregated data on labour force participation in environment-related economic activities in order to monitor employment trends, evaluate policy results, forecast changes needed in the current policy framework, and revise policies in line with' the transition to a low-carbon economy (section 3.2.4).
- Collect gender-disaggregated data on start-ups and innovative entrepreneurship to measure the impact of existing policies on gender equality and advance with additional or new measures (sections 2.4 and 3.2.1).
- Collect gender-disaggregated data and information on social considerations in environmental, climate and energy policies, such as on energy poverty by sex (section 2.2.1) and differentiated mobility patterns (section 2.3.1).
- Establish indicators to measure gender mainstreaming in environmental policies, women's participation in environmental leadership and decision-making, and women's economic empowerment through environmental economic activities (section 3.2.4).

References

OECD (2021), "Women in infrastructure: Selected stocktaking of good practices for inclusion of women in infrastructure", *OECD Public Governance Policy Papers*, No. 07, OECD Publishing, Paris, https://doi.org/10.1787/9eab66a8-en. [1]